THE PARANORMAL PRESIDENCY

of

Abraham

Lincoln

D1536745

Presentiments, Precognition, Prophetic Dreams, & Other Uncanny Encounters of the 16th President of the United States

Christopher Kiernan Coleman

4880 Lower Valley Road • Atglen, PA 19310

Designed by *Danielle D. Farmer*
Type set in P22 Cezanne Regular/Bookman Old Style/Edelsans

ISBN: 978-0-7643-4121-2
Printed in The United States of America

Published by Schiffer Publishing, Ltd.
4880 Lower Valley Road
Atglen, PA 19310
Phone: (610) 593-1777; Fax: (610) 593-2002
E-mail: Info@schifferbooks.com

For the largest selection of fine reference books on this and related subjects, please visit our website at: **www.schifferbooks.com.**
You may also write for a free catalog.

This book may be purchased from the publisher.
Please try your bookstore first.

We are always looking for people to write books on new and related subjects. If you have an idea for a book, please contact us at **proposals@schifferbooks.com.**

Schiffer Books are available at special discounts for bulk purchases for sales promotions or premiums. Special editions, including personalized covers, corporate imprints, and excerpts can be created in large quantities for special needs. For more information contact the publisher.

In Europe, Schiffer books are distributed by
Bushwood Books
6 Marksbury Ave.
Kew Gardens
Surrey TW9 4JF England
Phone: 44 (0) 20 8392 8585; Fax: 44 (0) 20 8392 9876
E-mail: info@bushwoodbooks.co.uk
Website: www.bushwoodbooks.co.uk

To my beloved wife Veronica...
Love is eternal

Acknowledgments

I would like to acknowledge the resources of the Tennessee State Library and Archives and assistance of its staff in researching this book, as well as that of the main branch of the Nashville Public Library. The explosive growth of online scholarly resources has also enabled access to archival material which would hitherto have required many months, if not years, of travel and study; notably the Library of Congress, the National Archives and the Internet Archive, as well as numerous other university resources online.

Contents

Introduction

Portrait of Lincoln taken by Alexander Gardner. This is believed to be one of the last photos taken of the President shortly before his death. His penetrating stare is usually interpreted by historians as a reflection of his strain of having guided the nation through four years of war. Is it instead the look of a man who has just seen his own funeral?

Saturday, April 22, 1865: The mood of the crowd in Philadelphia today is somber but charged with emotion. Thousands file past the open casket of their fallen leader, lying in state at Independence Hall.

All across the nation, citizens are grieving over the assassination of President Lincoln. Soon, in city after city, Lincoln's body will be waked for the sake of the grief-stricken multitude, but this day, in Philadelphia, there is a minor but significant difference to the wake.

As the throngs of mourners shuffle past the bier containing the body of the great man, a murmur arises along the line, as one object near the open casket catches the crowd's attention.

Juxtaposed between Lincoln's coffin and the Liberty Bell stands a memorial wreath; a casual glance reveals nothing exceptional about it. After all, hundreds such wreaths and garlands grace the hall this afternoon. It is no larger or more elaborate than any of the other memorials there. What catches the crowd's attention and stirs talk, rather, is the inscription emblazoned diagonally across it on a banner. It reads:

> *"Before every great national event I have always had the same dream.*
> *I had it the other night. It is of a ship sailing rapidly..."*[1]

For those shuffling through the hall, this cryptic phrase holds special meaning. For almost as fast as news spread that Lincoln was dead, word also spread that President Lincoln foretold his own death. The quote on the wreath repeats Lincoln's own words describing the prophetic dream he had the night before he died. Moreover, rumors spread that this prophetic dream of Lincoln's is no isolated incident.

In fact, Abraham Lincoln's whole career was punctuated with many such prophetic dreams, as well as portents, signs, and other uncanny events. When looked at as a totality, the distinct possibility arises that Abraham Lincoln, sixteenth president of the United States, may indeed have been endowed with paranormal gifts — far more so than any other known figure in American history.

Since time, immortal mankind has looked to his surroundings to discern what the future may portend. From dissecting the livers of sacred sheep, to charting the planets and stars, to observing the swirl of leaves in a grove of sacred trees, the systematic observation of omens and portents in nature — divination — may arguably be the world's *second* oldest profession.

Of old, rulers turned to such signs and wonders to guide them in their decision. The Great Kings of Babylon and Assyria had their diviners, Attila his shamans, Arthur his Merlin, and the Medieval Popes of Rome their Jewish astrologers. It should not seem so remarkable or incredible, therefore, to learn that modern leaders — even famous American presidents — have also had recourse on occasion to such sources of knowledge to sustain them as they sought to steer the ship of state through troubled waters to safety.

By and large, historians are a rational lot, not prone to wild speculation. Aside from a few popular writers on the subject, the majority of modern historians have chosen to draw a veil across Lincoln's relationship to paranormal belief and circumstance. Evidence that one of the nation's most important and revered political figures was guided in his career by dreams, omens, and visions has traditionally been greeted with skepticism and even outright disbelief by the academic community.

When confronted with sources that recite such paranormal incidents, scholars deem them "unreliable" or otherwise faulty; yet these very sources suddenly become reliable and accurate to the same researchers when they recount more mundane events in support of a pet theory about the President.

One of Lincoln's closest friends and unofficial bodyguard, Ward Hill Lamon, characterized Lincoln's belief in his personal destiny as a "vision of grandeur and of gloom" and insisted that it was a vision "which was confirmed in his mind by the dreams of his childhood, of his youthful days and of his mature years." Lincoln saw this vision, "of glory and of blood," with himself as the central figure.[2]

Abraham Lincoln is one of the most revered and highly regarded men in American History — and still the most written about. The fact that Lincoln was a pivotal figure in the history of our nation is undeniable; that Abraham Lincoln was a great leader and even greater humanitarian is also not in dispute; that Lincoln was also a man of the people is likewise a proposition that most experts could agree with. Yet, when one looks at some of the popular beliefs of the time to which Lincoln also subscribed, suddenly Lincoln experts develop a blind spot large enough to run a Conestoga wagon and team of oxen through. Lincoln was a man of his times and, like many of the "plain people" of his time, he possessed certain beliefs in the miraculous and supernatural that many modern intellectuals quite obviously do not share.

The fact that Lincoln believed in visions, dreams, presentiments, and other paranormal phenomena will be made abundantly clear in the following pages. In the ensuing chapter, we will document incidents that illumine Lincoln's paranormal beliefs as well as occurrences that served to confirm those beliefs. We will also show how all these not only affected his life and career, but also his wartime decisions as president.

A raking light will oft show details of a great painting not apparent from any other perspective. So too, will the following pages highlight those aspects of Abraham Lincoln and his presidency not otherwise seen in standard portraits of our sixteenth president.

Chapter 1

Whisperings of the Infinite

What were these wonderful presentiments? They were not the outpourings of a disordered brain. They came from minds thoroughly balanced, clear and strong — minds that worked with the precision of perfect machinery, even amid the excitement and fury of battle. They were not the promptings of an unmanly fear of danger or apprehension of death; for no men ever faced both danger and death with more absolute self-poise, sublimer courage, or profounder consecration.

Nor were these presentiments mere speculations as to chances. They were perceptions. There was about them no element of speculation. Their conspicuous characteristic was certainty. The knowledge seemed so firmly fixed that no argument as to possible mistake, no persuasion, could shake it. Where did that knowledge come from? It seems to me there can be but one answer, and that answer is another argument for immortality. It was the whispering of the Infinite beyond us to the Infinite within us — a whispering inaudible to the natural ear, but louder than the roar of battle to the spirit that heard it.

— General John Gordon (CSA)

The "cracked plate" Lincoln, believed to have been taken shortly before his death. His distant stare may be an indication that the President was experiencing a shallow altered state of consciousness at the time the photo was taken. Not only close friends, but even foreign visitors noted the ease with which Lincoln went in and out of such altered states.

Many a lengthy volume — indeed many, many volumes — have been penned about our beloved sixteenth President and his life and times. Some have focused on his humanism, others on his rationalism, and others portray him as a devout Christian. Still others have delved into the darker corners of his life, such as the issue of his paternity. There is hardly any aspect of Lincoln that has not come under minute scrutiny in the nearly century and a half since his passing.

Surprisingly, however, in the modern era, precious little serious study has been devoted to one aspect of Lincoln that was well-known to his contemporaries — his belief *in*, and possible encounters *with*, paranormal phenomena. Modern scholars and biographers, when confronted with the overwhelming evidence of Lincoln's beliefs in this area, have either discounted or chosen to ignore it.

While this present tome aims to remedy that deficiency, as we sift through the voluminous evidence for the sixteenth president's experiences in regard to the paranormal, it would be well to bear in mind that Lincoln's attitudes and beliefs in this area were by no means unique. Lincoln always regarded himself as a man of the people and even a cursory look at his life and times reveals ample evidence that he shared many popular notions about the supernatural that were common of that era.

Although Abraham Lincoln came to manhood in Indiana and Illinois, he was born in Kentucky and was a Southerner by birth; indeed, he was said to retain a slight Kentucky twang throughout his life.

In his autobiography, Lincoln jokingly describes himself as descended from the "second families" of Virginia. The log cabin in which he was born lay but a few miles distant from the log cabin Jefferson Davis was born in; as the two men grew, however, their families — and their politics — moved in opposite directions, but in origin both were Southern frontiersmen. Although Lincoln evolved intellectually, he still retained many of those core beliefs and attitudes of his early childhood.

Furthermore, much of the lands on both sides of the Ohio River were settled by folk migrating from the South. Even after secession, many people in southern Indiana and Illinois retained strong political sympathies for the South. Certainly their cultural values owed more to the Southern cultural tradition than to the New England cultural values more prevalent in the northern halves of these same states.[3]

Part of this Southern heritage in the Ohio Valley was a strong traditional belief in what some would call the supernatural. There was a significant Celtic flavor to Southern culture in general and along with this inheritance came a wide assortment of beliefs in the miraculous and the mystical that no God-fearing New England Puritan would ever adhere to. Whereas in the South — as in the Celtic lands of the British Isles — a "wise women" was held in respect and awe, in colonial New England they were more likely to be tortured and executed as a witch. William Herndon, Lincoln's law partner before the war, goes into some detail about the folk whom Lincoln grew up with and their beliefs:

> *"Although gay, prosperous, and light-hearted, these people were brimming over with superstition. It was at once their food and drink. They believed in the baneful influence of witches, pinned their faith in the curative powers of wizards in dealing with sick animals, and shot the image of a witch with a silver ball to break the spell she was supposed to have over human beings."*[4]

Nor was belief in witches the only notion in which the folk of Lincoln's boyhood subscribed to. They held a whole host of other popular beliefs and practices that we would more properly call paranormal or even occult. Virtually every rural community had its resident "water witch," or dowser, to divine sources of freshwater. Herndon informs us they "followed with religious minuteness the directions of the water-wizard, with his magic divining rod." Likewise, the "faith doctor" was far more common than a trained physician, "who wrought miraculous cures by strange sounds and signals to some mysterious agency."[5]

For the treatment of sick equine livestock, a "horse-whisperer" was frequently resorted to. Lincoln's benefactor and employer in New Salem, the "buoyant and effusive" Denton Offut, when his business ventures there came to naught there and he left town, resurfaced some years later in this capacity in Baltimore. Billing himself as a "veterinary surgeon and horse tamer," Offut professed "to have a secret to whisper in the horse's ear, or a secret manner of whispering in his ear," that was able to tame the wildest beast. Many a horse owner paid him the princely sum of five dollars for his services.[6]

Whatever Lincoln's attitude towards such folk practices may have been, we know for certain that Lincoln himself put great faith in the powers of madstones. In frontier communities innocent of orthodox medicine, people looked to traditional folk remedies to deal with maladies; the madstone was one such treatment. A madstone was a rock or stone believed to possess miraculous powers, able to cure rabies, and draw out the poison from snake bites.

Lincoln confided to a colleague in Illinois that "the people in the neighborhood of these stones [were] fully impressed with a belief in their virtues from actual experiment... and that was about as much as we could ever know about the properties of medicine." Significantly, when his oldest son Robert was bitten by a dog in Springfield, Lincoln rushed the boy to be treated by a madstone.[7]

The immigrants arriving to the thirteen colonies in the seventeenth and eighteenth centuries from the British Isles brought with them other folk beliefs as well. In addition to the above mentioned, their folklore included many other beliefs big and small involving the paranormal, including a whole host of "signs" or omens that could warn of coming misfortune: "the flight of a bird at the window, the breath of a horse on a child's head, the crossing by a dog of a hunter's path, all betokened evil luck in store for some one."[8]

Although the founding fathers of the United States were imbued with the spirit of the eighteenth century Enlightenment, the era in which Lincoln grew up was the age of Romanticism, which looked back towards the Middle Ages and its faith in the miraculous for its inspiration; it also put far greater stock in both folk culture and intuitive knowledge than the rationalists of the eighteenth century.

This included a widespread belief on both sides of the Atlantic in the reality of paranormal encounters. Charlotte Bronte, the famed nineteenth century novelist, succinctly expressed this general attitude in a passage in her best-selling novel, *Jane Eyre*: "Presentiments are strange things! And so are sympathies; and so are signs; and the three combined make one mystery to which humanity has not yet found the key."[9]

Signs and omens were everywhere in the society in which Lincoln passed his boyhood and young manhood. Indeed, the observation of signs in nature or in the heavens is a practice which goes back to antiquity. Even the bible frequently mentions signs and portents, which any devout reader of King James could hardly avoid and would provide ample justification for believing in their validity.

For the modern reader, Bronte's reference to presentiments and sympathies may be more obscure than her reference to signs, but for nineteenth century readers both terms would have been well understood — and believed in. Presentiments in particular were commonly referred to, not only in reference to Lincoln, but by many participants in the Civil War.

General John B. Gordon, CSA. Carte de Visite. President Lincoln was not the only person during the Civil War to have a presentiment of his own death; in fact there are many such documented cases, including Confederate General Gordon's brother, Lt. Col. Augustus Gordon, of the 6th Alabama Infantry. General Gordon described presentiments as the "whispering of the Infinite beyond us to the Infinite within us."

A *presentiment* originally meant a "previous conception, sentiment, opinion or apprehension." By the time of the Civil War, however, it had come to mean "an antecedent impression or conviction of something about to happen," similar to what would today be termed a premonition.[10]

While in theory one might have a presentiment of good fortune, "as their results are not tragical, they are seldom remembered....and for this reason the word presentiment is confined almost exclusively to inward premonitions of evil." Specifically, during the Civil War, it refers to one's own imminent death.[11]

During the war, there were numerous cases of soldiers who had presentiments and foretold them to their comrades. Confederate General John Gordon, who served with both Stonewall Jackson and D. H. Hill, informs us that "it would require a volume to record without comment the hundreds of such presentiments in both the Union and Confederate armies."[12]

A *sympathy*, in nineteenth century usage, was like a presentiment but referred to a preternatural awareness of an event as it was happening rather than occurring in the future. There are many anecdotes referring to a family member experiencing dread foreboding or extreme anxiety regarding an absent loved one, only to discover later that at the same time they had that sensation the person in question was indeed in great peril.

One member of the Lincoln administration and his spouse are known to have been firm believers in presentiments and sympathies: Ulysses S. Grant and his wife Julia Dent Grant.

Both their memoirs are peppered with references to the phenomena of presentiment and sympathy, as well as a belief in signs. One incident in particular serves as a striking example of a Civil War experience of such a preternatural sympathy.

On November 7, 1861, Julia Dent Grant was busy packing her trunks and valises in preparation for an anticipated visit with her husband, who was commanding the garrison at Cairo, Illinois. At that point in the war, southern Illinois was a hotbed of Rebel sympathizers and Cairo lay just across the river from the Rebel-held part of Missouri, so Grant was at a front-line post.

As Julia was in the midst of her preparations, an overwhelming sense of dread suddenly swept over her. Thinking she was coming down with some illness, Julia excused herself from a friend who was helping her pack and went upstairs to lie down until the spell passed. As Julia entered her bedroom, she saw before her the image of her husband. The vision of General Grant was vivid and real, although only his upper torso was visible and appeared suspended in mid-air. At that moment, Julia sensed her Ulysses was in grave danger. She let out a shriek and fainted.

As it turned out, at the exact same time that Julia had her uncanny vision, her husband Ulysses was leading a force in combat at Belmont, Missouri and was almost cut off from his retreating troops, coming very close to death or capture. When Julia was reunited with Ulysses, she related her vision to him. Grant replied: "That is singular. Just about that time, I was on horseback and in great peril, and I thought of you."[13]

Perhaps no aspect of Abraham Lincoln's relationship with the paranormal is as controversial as his involvement with séances and Spiritualism. At one extreme are those orthodox chroniclers who deny Lincoln had any dealings with séances, while at the other end are those Spiritualists — then and now — who claim the Great Emancipator as one of own.

Regardless of the merits of the conflicting claims, the fact is that to many of their contemporaries, the Lincolns attending séances would not have been regarded all that unusual. Certainly after the war, thousands of bereaved relatives resorted to the services of professional mediums to get in touch with a husband, son or brother lost in the conflict. Before the war, many Americans also attended séances. It was widely regarded as a form of entertainment, almost as a form of parlor game, and it was widely resorted to by Americans of education and status as well as common folk.

Signs, wonders, prescience, remote sensing, spirit visitation, psychokinesis, and a whole host of other paranormal phenomena were experienced by folks in America of varied stations and political views in the early nineteenth century. While later generations, in reflecting backwards, may have viewed such beliefs and practices as on the fringes of American society, clearly at the time they were not so regarded by a broad spectrum of Americans.

During and after the war, the paranormal encounters of Lincoln and his close associates were widely known by contemporaries. Many persons of Lincoln's day who considered themselves rational men believed firmly in such phenomena and subscribed to the notion that such phenomena were, in Confederate General Gordon's evocative phrase, "the whisperings of the Infinite beyond us to the Infinite within us."[14]

Chapter 2

A Rent in the Veil

"In his tenth year, he was kicked by a horse, and apparently killed for a time."
— *Abraham Lincoln, Autobiography (1860)*

Those who would treat honestly the character of Abraham Lincoln — rather than simply scribe yet another hagiography of him — must recognize two seemingly contradictory aspects of Lincoln's nature: On the one hand is Lincoln's well-known powers of reasoning — a side of the great man emphasized by almost all modern biographers. Indeed, one of Lincoln's close friends characterized him as an "intellect of mighty and exquisite mold...of a severely logical cast."[15] Yet Lincoln was also well-known to his contemporaries as a person who "believed also in the marvelous as revealed in presentiments and dreams."[16] Lincoln's close friend and partner, William Herndon, averred that Lincoln possessed a "superstitious view of life," which ran through his being, "like the thin blue vein through the whitest marble."[17]

Many of Lincoln's friends and associates attest to this dual nature of Abraham Lincoln's personality. While modern scholars have amply documented Lincoln's logical and rational side, the non-rational, intuitive aspects of Lincoln have generally been given short shrift by biographers and scholars, if not denied entirely. Whether Lincoln was indeed gifted with paranormal faculties or simply "superstitious," this side of the Great Emancipator was every bit as important as the "mathematical" part of his nature, perhaps even more so.

This being so, the question naturally arises as to how Lincoln's paranormal beliefs and experiences arose and became such an important part of his belief system. Those who knew him best all agree that it was not something that came to him late in life. Ward Hill Lamon, his friend and personal bodyguard during the war years, is clear on this point:

"From early youth he seemed conscious of a high mission. Long before his admission to the bar, or his entrance into politics, he believed that he was destined to rise to a great height....He also believed that from a lofty station he should fall."[18]

While Lincoln shared the beliefs of the "plain people," his preoccupation with supernatural phenomena was not some mere passive credulity or love of folklore. Rather, from his childhood through youth and on into his mature years, Lincoln experienced visions, intuitive insights, and prophetic dreams — all of which reinforced and verified his original beliefs on a very personal level.

Exactly when Lincoln first became aware of this "vision of glory and of blood" is not known, as even his close friends could not say when the recurring premonitions of his future fate first started coming to him or why. In recent decades, however, Lincoln researchers have identified one incident in his "early youth" that may well provide a partial answer to this question; although the inferences other Lincoln scholars have drawn about its lasting effects on him differ radically from ours.

Both psychiatrists and Lincoln scholars have identified an incident, mentioned by both Lincoln and his early biographers, that they feel caused "organic and emotional neuroses." As a child of ten, Lincoln suffered a severe blow to his head, which they feel affected the development of his personality and his career. A closer look at the incident may well reveal the medical experts' judgment to be true, but just not in the way they think.

When Lincoln was ten years old, his family was living in Gentryville, Indiana, which, at that time, was still thickly wooded wilderness. Although still young, his father had him in the woods almost every day, clearing trees for their farm. One chore that would take him away from this hard labor was the periodic trip to the mill to have their corn ground into meal.

Now this was not some tall windmill as one might see in the Low Countries or in New York; nor was it the more commonplace water mill with its giant vertical wheel that went round and round. No, this was but a humble little horse mill, a homemade affair where one would attach a dray animal that would slowly pace round and round in endless repetition till the dried corn was cracked and ground into something usable enough for bread or sour mash.

A local country gentleman named Gordon had gotten hold of some suitable stones and then fashioned the gears and spars and other parts out of wood. It was not the most efficient of mills; Lincoln once commented that his dog could eat the corn-meal that came out faster than the worn stones could grind it. Nor was Squire Gordon much of a Miller; each man brought his own horse to power it, did the grinding himself, and then paid the owner a tithe for the privilege. Still, it was the only mill that the good folk thereabouts had and if one wanted to have their daily bread, or corn whiskey, it was to Gordon's Mill that they repaired.

One day in 1818, Lincoln left the family cabin on Little Pigeon Creek and made his way the two miles to Gordon's Mill in the company of his friend David Turnham. Accompanying the pair was an unshod old gray mare and a sack of corn to be ground. Lincoln and Turnham arrived at the mill late in the day, so there were already several others there waiting their turn to use the mill. It was almost sundown when Lincoln was finally able to hitch his old flea-bitten nag to the wooden spar that turned the millstones. The two boys proceeded to pour the corn into the hopper, with Abe sitting astride the wooden arm as the horse slowly paced around in a circle.

If the mill was slow, the horse was even slower, so to goad the old girl into going faster, from time to time Lincoln would crack a small whip, adding a "Get up, you old hussy!" to further motivate the nag in its rounds.

Whether the gray mare resented the whip or the verbal insult to its honor more is not known; but it apparently did not take young Abe's blandishments kindly. On one revolution of the wooden arm, Lincoln began to shout out "Get up..." when suddenly the mare lifted its unshod rear hooves up and aimed them squarely at Lincoln's head. Young Abe went sprawling onto the ground.

Miller Gordon rushed up to the lifeless youth, who lay motionless and bleeding on the ground. Gordon picked up the bleeding body, but sensed no life in it. He sent word to the boy's father about the accident.

Old Thomas Lincoln arrived, apparently less grieved at his boy's fate than annoyed at the inconvenience. Old Thomas loaded up the body in his wagon and then slowly drove home, apparently resigned to the loss of a farmhand.

Abe was laid out in a bed, insensible to all stimuli; to all outward signs the boy was dead or close to it. All night long he lay there in bed, inanimate, pale, and lifeless. Curious neighbors came by the cabin to gawk at the prone figure. While death was common enough on the frontier, it never failed to evoke the interest of onlookers.

Towards daybreak, the mourners in the Lincoln household noticed that signs of life had started returning to the body of young Abe. Blood flowed back into his face and limbs, his tongue struggled to loosen as if trying to talk, and then his whole frame jerked for an instant — suddenly re-animated as if the soul had returned to the body. Abe woke with a start, blurting out "...you old hussy" — finishing the end of the sentence he'd started at the moment he'd been hit.[19]

Friends and associates testify that Lincoln always regarded the incident as singular. Herndon tells us that he and Lincoln discussed the "psychological phenomena" involved in the incident several times. A number of serious Lincoln researchers have similarly discussed the psychological consequences of Lincoln's injury and offered their theories as to how it affected his later life.

Analysis of photos of the adult Lincoln, as well as his life and death masks, have indeed verified that Lincoln suffered a severe blow to the forehead over the left eye, likely fracturing the skull at the point of impact. Judging from the size and depth of the depression left on his skull, medical experts aver that it was clearly life-threatening.

At least one medical expert has theorized that Lincoln suffered brain damage from the head wound. Specifically, the frontal lobe of his brain received a severe injury; this same researcher concluded that the "most significant of all symptoms," of this brain injury, was "the repetitive tendency to lapse automatically into a lower consciousness state of mental detachment or abstraction." Another investigator diagnosed his condition as Marfan's Syndrome, which is sometimes referred to as "petit mal."[20]

Lincoln's "occult" condition (Herndon's phrase) these psychiatric experts have interpreted as schizoid and neurotic symptoms due to the injury. While we may dispute Lincoln's "occult" behavior as a form of mental illness, we may certainly agree that Lincoln experienced repeated alternate states of consciousness — not "lower" states but rather higher states of consciousness. Even today, the nature of such states is much disputed; not surprisingly Lincoln's contemporaries, while aware of this aspect of Lincoln's personality, understood it according to the culture of the time. William Herndon expressed it in this way:

> "Mr. Lincoln was a peculiar, mysterious man — had a double consciousness, a double life. The two states, never in a normal man, coexist in equal and vigorous activities though they succeed each other quickly. One state predominates and, while it so rules, the other state is somewhat quiescent, shadowy, yet living, a real thing. This is the sole reason why Lincoln so quickly passed from one state of consciousness to another and a different state."[21]

Visiting Lincoln in 1865, the Marquis de Chambron similarly observed the President passing into shallow altered states late in the war: "I saw him...abstract himself completely, as though absorbed in deep meditation." In one evening alone, the Marquis observed Lincoln go into such states multiple times.[22]

Lincoln's near-death experience as a boy clearly seems to have been the event that led to his frequent shallow alterations in consciousness, sometimes interpreted as "melancholy." However, it may well be that this same near-death encounter also caused more profound altered states of consciousness, which would have a serious affect on his life and career.

In recent decades, more and more information has come to light about the phenomenon of near death experience (or NDE). A number of individuals who were declared clinically dead and revived have described out-of-body experiences or believe that they were on the verge of being led into the afterlife in the form of a bright light. Persons who have had near-death experiences have also been reported to have four times the number of paranormal experiences as the population at large. Prophetic dreams, visions, and other psychic phenomena — as well as a general sense of renewed belief in having a mission or purpose in life — are commonly reported as lasting effects of such experiences, especially in those with injury to the front temporal lobes of the brain.[23]

Anthropologists, looking at similar phenomena from a different perspective, have also provided evidence as to the causative nature of altered states as they pertain to paranormal encounters. Anthropologists have long studied Shamanism as a world-wide phenomenon. Shamans, sometimes referred to as "witch doctors" or medicine men, are persons who are believed to possess paranormal powers, such as the ability to foresee the future or cure physical or spiritual ailments, and who are in close contact with the spirit world through dreams, visions, and altered states of consciousness.

While studying shamans, anthropologists and students of comparative religions have observed certain common factors in how one is summoned to become a shaman: commonly a person suffers a life-threatening disease accompanied by high fever or else undergoes a severe head injury that also brings them close to death. They emerge from such traumas with the belief that they have been summoned to the vocation of the shaman. As Western researchers have theorized about near death experiences in general, one theory about such individuals is that the near death trauma affects the temporal lobes of the brain, in some way stimulating those parts of their brain involved with intuitive knowledge and abilities that we commonly call paranormal.

While no one would dare claim that Lincoln was on a par with some native dancing around a fire and chanting magic incantations, it may well be that the psychological and physiological factors involved with Lincoln's brush with death had a similar effect on him. That Abraham Lincoln suffered a traumatic head injury and came very near death is beyond doubt, but how and to what extent he was afflicted by this injury remains a matter of speculation.

As we review the evidence for Lincoln's paranormal beliefs and experiences, without discounting the medical testimony entirely, we should also keep in mind this alternative explanation. Certainly this early incident in Lincoln's life and its consequences need to be kept in mind, for it is entirely likely that this was what first caused Lincoln "a rent in the veil which hides from mortal view what the future holds" and which throughout the rest of his life "elated and alarmed" him.[24]

Chapter 3

Voodoo Child

"I heard the singing of the Mississippi
When Abe Lincoln went down to New Orleans.
I've seen its muddy bosom turn all gold in the sunset."
— Langston Hughes, A Negro Talks of Rivers (1921)

Langston Hughes was only a teenager when he wrote his famous poem. It is said it came upon him all of a sudden; in his flash of inspiration, African Americans were inextricably intertwined with both the Mississippi and Lincoln. Like Hughes, Abraham Lincoln was but a teenager when he gazed upon the Mississippi in all its glory. In Lincoln's case, however, the flash of insight came not while viewing the river, but after arriving at the goal of his voyage — New Orleans.

The Choctaw called it mishi-pokni sipikina — "He whose age is beyond counting" — but the Choctaw's slaves simplified it to the more evocative "Old Man River" while Whites, hearing the native phrase, garbled it into the name Mississippi. Whether North or South, the Mississippi was the heart's blood of the Western United States. During the early days of the Republic, long before the Civil War, lack of American control of the great river brought the Westerners to the brink of secession.

Even in the backwoods of Indiana, the many tributaries of the Mississippi branched deep into the everyday life of the rural folk there like the pulsing arteries of some great creature. Up until 1828, Lincoln's view of the world was circumscribed by the farms and small town merchants of Gentryville; the Sangamon was all Lincoln had ever seen of rivers.

Lincoln's first view of the wider world came at the behest of James Gentry, for whom Abe had done work before. The latter gentleman outfitted a flatboat, filled it to the brim with grain, meat, and other trade goods, put his son Allen in charge, and recruited Abe as bow-hand.

In March 1828, young Abe Lincoln began his odyssey. Little is known of this first voyage, save that Abe and Gentry had a run-in with a band of African American river pirates while tied up to Duchesne Plantation a few miles below Baton Rouge. The marauders did not realize that young Abe Lincoln, armed with an axe handle, was a force to be reckoned with and beat a hasty retreat.

The crew of two sold their cargo in New Orleans for a profit and, after an undetermined amount of time enjoying the fleshpots of the Crescent City, headed back to Indiana. Little is known of what transpired in the Big Easy on this first voyage of Lincoln's, perhaps deliberately so.[25]

The plaster death mask made soon after the Great Emancipator died was but the first layer of successive coats of plaster lain over the great man's image. Since then, successive biographers have striven mightily to turn the man Lincoln into a secular saint. Even William Herndon, criticized by many of Lincoln's friends for being too indiscreet in his three-volume biography, suppressed a great deal of information he had gathered about Lincoln that he thought might have cast his friend in a less than favorable light.[26]

One recent academic study of Lincoln's voyages to New Orleans claims that while the virile young men were in the middle of the most decadent fleshpot in Dixie that Abe and Allen Gentry "probably" did not visit the city's infamous red light district known as "the Swamp." Instead, the historian

theorizes that Lincoln spent his time reading newspapers and learning about the politics of the day![27]

While it is true that Lincoln was not a drinking man, Herndon's unpublished notes provide substantial evidence that Lincoln's "shyness in the company of women" was largely a fabrication created to sanitize the slain President's image. While we may question Herndon's gossipy sources about Lincoln begetting bastards, in 1828, certainly, Abraham Lincoln was a healthy young man with the same overabundance of male hormones as any male his age. While we can't be certain Lincoln frequented any houses of ill repute during his time in the Big Easy, if he had done so he would not have been in any way different than many a backwoodsman of the era who came to market to sell their goods.

Similarly, New Orleans of this era was well-known as a hotbed of magical practices; after all, Voodoo ceremonies were openly practiced in public. The live performances in Congo Square, where African American priestesses danced nude (or nearly so) to the rhythm of wild African drums, were in fact a major source of entertainment for visitors to the city in its heyday. Even if Abe and Allen Gentry had spent but a few days there on this first trip, they could not have failed to have been exposed to some aspect of New Orleans' active Voodoo culture.

As to young Abe Lincoln's second sojourn to New Orleans in 1831, we are far better informed. This time around, Lincoln went at the behest of Denton Offut, "a brisk and venturesome businessman." Offut initially recruited John Hanks to take a boatload of stock and provisions down to New Orleans; Hanks, in turn, convinced Offut to also hire Lincoln and his step-brother John Johnson for the expedition.

The three young men met up with Offut in an establishment in the young town of Springfield known as the Buckhorn Inn. Passing beneath the painted sign of a horned stag that swayed back and forth over the entrance, the trio found Offut seriously engaged in sampling the inn's liquid refreshments. Offut was supposed to have had a flatboat ready for them, but his daily libations at the Buckhorn had somehow interfered with those intentions. Instead, the three young voyagers had to build the boat themselves.

After four weeks of work, the boat was launched, loaded with barrels of pork, sacks of corn, and livestock. Once clear of the local mill dam on the Sangamon River, the boat made steady progress, first down the Ohio and thence on down the Mississippi. Lincoln and his shipmates arrived in New Orleans in early May 1831.

After disposing of the cargo on behalf of their sponsor, the three young men lingered in the Crescent City for a month, "viewing the sights" in which the city had to offer young men with money in their pockets. Again, we may seriously question whether young Abe Lincoln whiled away the time reading newspapers and arguing the politics of the day as his biographers would have us believe. We do know that Lincoln experienced at least two events on this trip that would profoundly affect his future career.

During his early boyhood in

Kentucky, Lincoln had certainly seen slaves at some point, but there, where farmers were mostly small freeholders, the landowners generally owned one or two slaves. The slaves served as either field hands whose labor was in addition to that of the farmer's sons and worked side-by-side with them or as additional domestic labor to help the farmer's wife with her chores. The slaves were not the farm's sole source of labor, but a supplement to the farmer's own efforts. Lincoln had never really witnessed first-hand the full horrors of slavery and the slave trade before.

In New Orleans in 1831, for the first time in his life Lincoln came face-to-face with a slave market. He saw African Americans in chains, whipped and scourged. He also saw families head to market to be sold — husband from wife, children from parents — never to see one another again. One morning in their rambles around town, the trio came across one such auction in progress. It was of a young, light-skinned slave girl, "vigorous and comely," in the process of being sold to the highest bidder. The prospective buyers grabbed her all over her body and made her trot up and down to see how she moved. It was obvious that the bidders had something more than manual labor in mind for her. The sight outraged Lincoln.

"By God, boys, let's get away from this," said Lincoln. "If ever I get a chance to hit that thing (slavery), I'll hit it hard."

As John Hanks later commented, "Slavery ran the iron into him then and there."[28]

Sometime during that same month,

Lincoln had another experience that impressed him greatly. Lincoln paid a visit to an elderly black fortune-teller — an "old voodoo negress." The fact that Lincoln would have his fortune told was in no way exceptional; it was one of the more benign activities in which Voodoo practitioners engaged and was a popular diversion for visitors to the city then as it is now.

In the course of the session, this ebony Sibyl went into a trance, emitting a series of more or less generic predictions. Soon, though, she became particularly excited, exclaiming to Lincoln in particular: "You will be president, and all the Negroes will be free!"[29] While fortune-tellers are notorious for being able to give a "cold reading" and tell patrons what they wish to hear, it was exceptional that this "voodoo seer should utter a prophecy that was so specific — and one so in line with Lincoln's own current train of thought."

Lincoln, as we've seen, already had the implicit belief that he was destined for some great purpose in life. There is little doubt that this second voyage to New Orleans, where he first realized both the true malicious nature of slavery and the subsequent injunction laid upon him by the Voodoo seer, had a profound effect on the impressionable young woodsman.

We have it on the authority of his close friend John Hanks how deeply the visit influenced him. "His heart bled," Hanks told one biographer. "He was mad, thoughtful, abstracted, sad, and depressed." Lincoln's deeply felt opposition to slavery clearly dates to this time; his belief that it was his life's pre-ordained mission to end this evil undoubtedly dates to this voyage as well.[30]

In the fall of 1864, before Lincoln's re-election, where the issue of Union or Disunion was to be settled by the presidential election, Lincoln again paid a visit to a "black prophetess" in nearby Georgetown. The fortune-teller is described as a "Voodoo Woman," although she was more likely a practitioner of Hoodoo, Voodoo's more widespread country cousin. Regardless, we are informed that "like King Saul in the Bible, he asked about his future." The oracle went into a nearby darkened room "to raise up mystic spirits and speak with them" and then returned to the consultation parlor to give Lincoln his answer: "General Grant will capture Richmond, you will be next president...

but beware of Chase!"[31]

While it is easy enough for modern biographers to explain away the Voodoo fortune-tellers' prophecies, Lincoln, at least, put great stock in them. One may argue they simply served to confirm attitudes and beliefs already deeply ingrained in Lincoln's psyche rather than set him on a whole new course. From this perspective, they may be viewed more as affirmations than prophecies. Nonetheless, they did come true.

One thing is certain about the youthful Abe after his voyages down the Mississippi: As a result of his sojourns, young Mr. Lincoln could truly say — as young Langston Hughes did in his poem — "my soul has grown deep like the river."

Chapter 4

Abraham and Mary: Partners in Prophecy

"*He is to be President of the United States some day;
if I had not thought so I never would have married him.*"

— Mary Todd Lincoln

Mary Todd Lincoln, soon after her marriage. Mary believed from childhood that she would one day be First Lady. The first time she met young lawyer Lincoln, she knew he was destined to be President.

Abraham Lincoln, prairie lawyer. Although a struggling young lawyer and a relative unknown in politics, he, like his wife, believed he was destined by fate to rise to the highest office in the land.

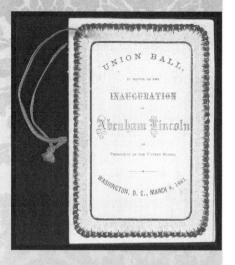

Dance Card, Inaugural Ball, March, 1861. As a young girl, Mary Todd dreamed that one day she would dance at a cotillion in the White House. Her dreams, like her husband's, proved prophetic. *Bottom photo, courtesy of the Library of Congress.*

When historians take note of Lincoln's relationship to the paranormal — if they do at all — they have a convenient scapegoat close at hand in which to dismiss any serious consideration of Lincoln's involvement with anything supernatural: Mary Todd Lincoln. In fact, just about any negative aspect of the Lincoln Presidency has been put at the foot of Mr. Lincoln's First Lady at one time or another.

This critique of Mary Todd Lincoln is not of late date. Almost from the day she passed the portals of the White House, Mary Lincoln came in for a torrent of verbal abuse and criticism. Born and raised an upper class Southern woman, the social aristocracy of Washington, overwhelmingly secessionist in sentiment, widely regarded Mary as a traitor to her class and region. Moreover, these same snobby Virginia Swans who ran Washington society also looked down on Mary as an uncouth Westerner lacking in social graces.[32]

Northerners, particularly the militant Radical Republican politicians, regarded her as a covert secessionist sympathizer and traitor to the Union. The fact that many of Mary's relatives actually were Confederate soldiers buttressed their claims of her being an agent for the Confederacy. Gossip and rumors about the First Lady soon blossomed into outright lies and calumnies. In truth, Mary was never very good at holding her tongue. A female cousin of Mary's once described her personality as "like a spring day." Even in youth, Miss Todd was liable to outbursts "like a sudden spring thunderstorm, but then the anger would pass and Mary would be all sunny once more."

In Washington, then as it is now, honesty and candor were not highly regarded virtues and Mary was rarely able to disguise her feelings. She was outspoken in an age when women were expected to hold their tongue. Well-educated and cultured when most men were not and raised amid wealth and privilege, she often spent beyond her husband's means. Moreover, her sense of entitlement and vanity left her vulnerable to flattery by sycophants seeking favors of the White House.

It was all too easy, therefore, for post-war biographers seeking to turn Lincoln into a secular saint to also demonize Mary Todd Lincoln as a selfish, neurotic, shrewish spouse and portray Lincoln as her patient but long-suffering husband. For those whom Lincoln's interest in the uncanny and paranormal was considered a negative trait, it was a simple thing to blame his wife for any inconvenient truths regarding the President.

Abraham and Mary's relationship, both with the paranormal and with each other, is far more complex than many Lincoln biographers have been willing to concede. To gain a clear insight into Lincoln's involvement with the supernatural, we must first come to some understanding of the relationship between Mary and Abraham — a "power couple" if ever there was one.

Even if one does not believe in destiny or the power of fate, the law of averages were certainly on Mary Todd's side that she would one day become First Lady. No less than three of the four men who campaigned for president of the United States in 1860 had, at one time or another, courted Miss Todd. There was Abraham Lincoln, the Republican; Stephen Douglas, the "Little Giant," the candidate for the Northern Democrats; and John C. Breckenridge of Kentucky, the candidate of the Southern Democrats. A coincidence it may be, but a most uncanny one.

On the face of it, there would seem to be no more a mismatched couple than Abraham Lincoln and Mary Todd. Abe's humble origins, his lack of formal education, the series of low-paying odd jobs, and his career as backwoods lawyer and politician are all well known and have become the stuff of legends. When Abe was first introduced to Miss Todd, he was lacking in social graces and both his financial and political prospects seemed dim.

By contrast, Mary Todd had been born into a distinguished Kentucky family. Robert Todd, her father, was not only wealthy, but well-connected politically, and if Mr. Todd was generally too busy to give Mary his personal attention, he spared no material luxuries on her behalf. She was educated by Madame Mentelle, of Lexington, who taught her students entirely in French; Mary was equally fluent in French or English. French, it should be understood, was the lingua franca of international diplomacy in those days. Mary was later "finished" at Mrs. Ward's Academy, a prestigious school for young ladies of quality. Young Mary Todd was in fact better educated than most adult men of her era.

Full-figured and petite, Mary was considered attractive by the standards of the day, but more importantly, she could be charming, witty, and very personable when she so chose. Even William Herndon, who generally had little good to say of Mary, observed that when she arrived in Springfield, Illinois, "her trenchant wit, affability, and candor pleased the young men, not less than her culture and varied accomplishments impressed the older ones with whom she came into contact."[33] Her father's wealth and political influence no doubt further added to her attractiveness as a potential mate. In short, Mary Todd was everything that Abraham Lincoln was not.

Nevertheless, when the two met, something strange happened. Mary, who could have had the pick of the most eligible bachelors in either Kentucky or Illinois, set her sights on the bumpkin lawyer Lincoln — "a poor nobody," in his own words. Introduced to Mary by a lawyer friend of Lincoln's, Lincoln was immediately charmed by her wit and beauty. In her sister's drawing room in Springfield, Lincoln would visit Mary, with Miss Todd doing most of the talking. Lincoln was deep in the spell of this Southern belle; curiously, Mary seemed equally enthralled by this rugged, awkward young man.

Friends and relatives of both Mary and Abe remarked how ill-suited they seemed for each other. Yet something deeper than either reason or circumstance could explain was going on between the twain. Mrs. Ninian Edwards, Mary's older sister, observed that Lincoln "gazed on her as if irresistibly drawn towards her by some superior and unseen power."[34]

We know that Lincoln had his "vision of power and glory" from an early age and that his sense of destiny had been refined and defined by his trips to New Orleans, but there is absolutely no evidence to indicate that during their courtship Lincoln ever shared his prophetic insights with Miss Todd. Even if he had, this elegant young belle could hardly have been expected to give credence to his lofty visions, given Lincoln's modest circumstances. Nonetheless, there is good reason to believe that from the very moment Mary set eyes on Lincoln she believed without question that he would someday become president — and that she never wavered in this intuitive knowledge throughout their long years of struggle together.

While cynics (and Herndon) might well argue that Lincoln was attracted to Mary Todd as a mate whose social and political connections would further his career ambitions, from a purely practical point of view it remains difficult to see what Mary saw in Lincoln. However, Mary's older sister Elizabeth tells us that Mary said "when a girl, to her friends in Kentucky, that she was destined to marry a president." Elizabeth avers that Mary said so "in Kentucky often and often" and also "said it in my presence in Springfield and said it in earnest."[35] Mary repeated that "seemingly absurd and idle boast."[36] Mary is also reported to have dreamed of dancing in the White House at a cotillion as a child. It seems Mr. Lincoln was not the only one to have prophetic dreams and presentiments.

That Miss Mary Todd was "social and loved glitter show and pomp and power" and "was an extremely ambitious woman" is not to be doubted.[37] The fact remains, however, that when Mary first met Abraham, no one but Mary saw a prospective presidential candidate in the ungainly and awkward prairie lawyer.

Elizabeth Todd Edwards' comments about her sister's innate belief — perhaps prophetic faith — in Lincoln is confirmed by another of Lincoln's close friends: Ward Hill Lamon. Only a few months after meeting Lincoln, Lamon attended a reception held at the Lincolns' home in Springfield. After Abe introduced Ward to his wife, he left them alone to converse.

Lamon was making idle chatter to Mary about her husband's popularity. Lincoln was at that time still a hard-working solicitor, hardly known beyond eastern Illinois. Yet Mary blurted out, "Yes, he is a great favorite everywhere. He is to be President of the United States someday; if I had not thought so I never would have married him, for you can see he is not pretty."[38]

Lamon, only lately an acquaintance of Lincoln's, was taken aback by Mary's bold pronouncement. "I felt convinced that Mrs. Lincoln was running Abraham beyond his proper distance." In fact, time would justify Mary's faith in her husband; but at the time it seemed a bold, if not to say bizarre, pronouncement to Ward Lamon.

Today nobody talks much about "women's intuition" anymore, although one would wager many women still make important decisions based on it. Mary's own intuition in seeking Lincoln as a mate was clearly not based on any pragmatic considerations. Rather, some inner voice told the ambitious Miss Todd that this unlikely candidate for her hand in marriage would one day be president of the United States and that if she were to fulfill her destiny to latch hold of him and not let go. It was an inner knowledge that she could not explain, devoid of logic or empirical cause.

One can try to rationalize Mary Todd's behavior in any number of ways, but intuition remains the best explanation of Mary's reaction on meeting Abe for the first time when he came up to her at a cotillion and said to her, "Miss Todd, I want to dance with you in the worst way." Something deep inside her whispered to Mary that this man would be president some day. Informed by her inner voice, Mary then focused all her not inconsiderable feminine powers of charm, grace, and persuasion on winning his heart. While their courtship has been described as "stormy," Mary persisted despite all logic, until she had attained her heart's desire.

Biographers have made much of Lincoln's uncertain courtship of Mary; yet they have never adequately explained how a woman so proud and quick to temper would have put up with repeated slights from any man, much less from the poor country lawyer as Lincoln was at the time. Mary's patience in all this can only be fathomed if we accept her absolute certainty that this gawky bumpkin lawyer in his ill-fitting clothes would one day ascend to the highest office in the land.

Having secured her heart's desire, Mary never once wavered in her faith in her husband's destiny: "She loved power and prominence, and when she occasionally came down to our office, it seemed to me then that she was inordinately proud of her tall and ungainly husband. She saw in him bright prospects ahead, and his every move was watched by her with the closest interest."[39] Lincoln's friend, Lamon, confirms that from the time he met Mary to the day of her husband's inauguration she "never wavered in her faith that her hopes in this respect would be realized."[40]

We know that the Lincoln's marriage was quite different from the Victorian norm. Whereas wives were supposed to be docile and not speak up, Mary Todd Lincoln gained a reputation for outspoken opinions; also atypically, Lincoln often paid heed to his wife's counsel: "My husband placed great reliance of my knowledge of human nature, often telling me, when about to make some important appointment, that he had no knowledge of men and their motivations."[41]

Although more sophisticated and better educated than her husband, Mary nonetheless shared many of his values and beliefs when it came to the paranormal. While it has been customary for biographers to place all such things upon Mary alone, it seems clear that here, as in many aspects of his career, there was a dynamic psychic symbiosis between Abraham Lincoln and his spouse.

In some of the better documented paranormal incidents of Lincoln's life, it often transpired that it would be Lincoln who would experience something uncanny — be it disturbing dream, ominous omen, or the like — and then tell his wife about it. Even if he did not verbalize it, Mary, closely attuned to her husband's state of mind, would notice something was wrong and try to pry out of him the cause.

Lincoln would begin to tell her of his presentiment or vision and just as quickly drop the subject, tying to minimize its significance or dismiss it as unimportant. This, of course, only upset Mary even more and, like any wife, would not rest until Abe had told her fully about the incident. In almost every case, it was Abraham, not Mary, who was the instigator.

We may also observe that, while it was Lincoln who had the uncanny experience, it was his wife who was often left to interpret it. By the time they took up abode in the White House, Abraham and Mary had been married for many years and she was long-acquainted with her husband's prophetic, maybe even "superstitious," turn of mind. No doubt there were many more such incidents that transpired in the earlier years that Abe had shared with Mary since their union in 1842 than were ever committed to paper.

One cannot deny that Mary Todd Lincoln had her character flaws or that, like any married couple, she and her husband had their domestic spats, but more than any other person in Lincoln's life, she was the active participant in helping her husband achieve what both believed to be his destiny. Looking at Mary's intimate relationship with her husband's paranormal beliefs and experiences, it is almost impossible to avoid the conclusion that Mary and Abraham were partners in prophecy.

Chapter 5

Through the Looking Glass

"It's a poor sort of memory that only works backwards."

— Lewis Carroll

The road to the White House proved a long one for Abraham Lincoln. Although neither Abe nor Mary ever wavered in their conviction regarding his ultimate destiny, the path to the presidency was neither simple nor straight.

Abe served but one term as congressman from Illinois and, while he obtained some national exposure, circumstance prevented a second term. At one point, Abe had been offered the post of territorial governor of Oregon, but on Mary's advice he turned it down. Fate, Mary felt, had greater things in store for her husband.

Lincoln began his political career as a member of the Whig Party, but that political faction died a little mourned death; in its stead, the Republican Party rose from the ashes, merging Whigs, Free Soil Democrats, and others dissatisfied with the status quo. Lincoln, however, was not their first choice for president: in 1856 they nominated John C. Fremont, famed explorer, hero of the Mexican War, and abolitionist hailing from South Carolina.

Nevertheless, as Abe had done in his law practice, Lincoln, bit by bit, gained wider recognition, even as the nation became more politically fractured over the issue of slavery and its extension into the Western territories. By 1860, therefore, Lincoln's time had come at last.

In 1860, the Democratic Party split in twain along geographic lines, with the Southern Democrats pushing a militant pro-slavery platform in the guise of "states rights" and the Northern Democrats supporting "free choice" in the territories but not willing to back the radical agenda of the Southern militants. In the middle was John Bell of Tennessee's Union Party, which vaguely emphasized national unity and compromise over sectional rivalries.

The Republicans, while portrayed by secessionists as threatening their precious "Southern rights," in fact recognized the constitutional right to own slaves and were not even opposed to the Fugitive Slave provisions of the constitution. However, Republicans generally saw slavery as a moral evil and opposed extending that evil into the new Western territories. They, Lincoln included, condemned John Brown's raid at Harper's Ferry and any similar violent acts.

The truth is that in 1860 actual abolitionists in the North were a small but vocal minority and posed little real threat to the institution of slavery. However, by November of that year, militants south of the Mason-Dixon Line had largely stopped listening to anyone but themselves. By the time Election Day rolled around, secessionists had drawn a line in the sand and even if the North chose not to step over it, they aimed to make the South do it.

November 6, 1860 — Election Day — finds Abraham Lincoln spending most of the day at his offices in Springfield as if it is a normal working day. Around three in the afternoon, Lincoln strolls over to the polling place at the courthouse. A multitude is there already, mostly supporters gathering to cheer on Springfield's favorite son. Hands are stretched forth to shake Lincoln's and talk to him, but the crush of the crowd is too great for Abe to give them individual attention. Inside the courthouse, Abe cuts his own name off the ballot and then votes straight along the party line.

After doing his duty at the polls, Lincoln returns to his office in the State House and resumes meeting with select visitors and clients. After the polls close, Lincoln walks over to the telegraph office to check on incoming returns.

Thanks to the telegraph, news these days arrives far faster than it used to. Where before electoral returns could take weeks, now the magic of electro-magnetic communications speeds results in from all across the nation in a matter of days. Lincoln stays at the telegraph office, his unofficial campaign headquarters, until it closes at midnight. Shortly after the witching hour, Abe and Mary attend to supper and then go home.

By next morning, the electoral returns are coming in with ever greater rapidity. District by district, state by state, the news of who is ahead and who is behind changes hour by hour; Lincoln spends most of the day at the Springfield telegraph office, closely following the results of the race.

As each state falls in line behind Lincoln, a shout of "hurrah, boys!" wells up from Lincoln's supporters gathered around the telegraph office. Finally, by 4:45 p.m., the results coming in from all quarters are clear: Abraham Lincoln will become the Sixteenth President of the United States.

From the telegraph office, Lincoln proceeds over to the state capitol's House chambers, where he makes a brief statement announcing victory. "We expected it would be so," he tells the crowd, "and so it is."[42]

Although Lincoln's demeanor is outwardly placid, in fact the two days' of closely following polling returns, combined with the prior strain of campaigning, are finally taking its toll.

Exhausted, Lincoln returns home to his chambers, where he throws himself down on a lounge.

Lying there, mentally at peace for perhaps the first time in many weeks, Lincoln stares idly across the room at a bureau, to which is affixed a large swivel mirror. The looking-glass is sufficiently large that he can see nearly his whole long, lanky figure reflected there.

Perhaps it is the quiet of the room that puts him into a meditative state or simply sheer physical exhaustion, but after a time, staring blankly into the looking glass, Lincoln notices something strange about his image reflected there. Peering more closely, he notices that his face — and his face alone — has "two separate and distinct images." Discussing it later with friends, Abraham is quite specific about the double image: "The tip of the nose of one being...three inches from the tip of the other."[43]

This dual image startles Lincoln. He gets up and walks over to inspect the mirror. As Lincoln rises from his prone position, however, the image disappears.

Lincoln lies back on the couch as before. Settling in, he again sees the Janus-like vision of his face reflecting back at him in the looking glass "plainer, if possible, than before."

This time Lincoln observes that one of the faces is paler — "say five shades" paler than the other. Again, as soon as Abe gets up from his relaxed position, "the thing" melts away. Unable to rest with this disturbing vision before him, Lincoln gets up and leaves his private room. Before long, Lincoln is deeply enmeshed in the post-election frenzy.

For a time, the incident of the dual image in the looking glass is pushed out of Lincoln's mind by more mundane matters. Lincoln tells us that he forgets about the incident "nearly, but not quite." He confesses that "the thing" would once in a while come up and give him "a little pang, as though something uncomfortable had happened."[44]

Clearly, the incident bothered Lincoln quite a bit more than "a little" since he mentions it to at least two people nearly four years later, in 1864, during his re-election campaign and then to a third person shortly after his re-election.[45] While the three informants differ on particulars, there is no doubt that the incident actually happened to Lincoln — or that it made a profound impression on the President.

Of course, there was a fourth person whom Lincoln confided the vision of the Looking Glass to — his wife Mary. Soon after it occurred, Abe described the "illusion" to Mary. By this time Mary was only too well aware of Lincoln's prophetic visions and dreams, and she became quite concerned.

Though Lincoln is able to reproduce the dual image in the looking glass a few days after the first incident, he is apparently unable to ever duplicate the effect for the benefit of his wife Mary, giving a lie to the rationale that it was a mere optical effect. Mary is all the more concerned when Abe's optical experiment fails.

As is commonly the case, it is Mary who is able to interpret this "sign" to Lincoln: To Mary, it is clear that the life-like image in the looking glass means that Abraham will serve all the way through his first term; the paler image means that he will be re-elected, but his ghostly visage betokens that

he will not live to see the end of his second term.

Lincoln's rational side wants to believe this double image is merely some optical illusion. However, as one friend observes, "the flavor of superstition which hangs about every man's composition made him wish he had never seen it."[46] Several of those close to Lincoln cannot help but believe that "the thing" is a warning of death.

How is one to interpret this incident? Is it a presentiment of death, is it "by his interpretation a premonition of impending doom?" Or is it "but an optical illusion, the natural result of some principle of refraction or optics which I did not understand?"[47]

Since Lincoln's passing, both schools of thought have weighed in on this incident. The professional debunkers — cynics who have made a career out of imposing their own prejudices and preconceptions on phenomena and presenting them as objective truth — have seemingly made short work of this particular paranormal event of Lincoln's. One debunker took aim at the incident and has published his opinion about it. He claims to have re-created the effect, declaring it nothing more than an easily explained imperfection common in old mirrors.[48]

However, it is a scientific fact the glass is not a solid but a fluid; over time all glass will lose its shape due to the pull of gravity. Thus, any old mirror after a century and a half will likely have flaws and imperfections in it. By carefully manipulating an old couch and mirror, it's probable that some sort of distortion will result. If one then is highly selective in choosing one's antique mirror, one certainly can claim success — sort of.

Ever since Harry Houdini, professional debunkers have followed a certain methodology in their efforts to disprove what they don't wish to believe. Houdini, a master illusionist, would replicate an alleged phenomenon artificially; once having done so using modern technology, he would then declare to the world "this is how they faked it."

It is quite true, to give the devil his due, that wherever there is opportunity for gain there is also a chance for chicanery present. It is also a general principle that almost any process — natural or supernatural — can be mimicked by modern technology in some fashion or other. As Arthur C. Clarke has observed, "Any sufficiently advanced technology is indistinguishable from magic." However, a zircon is not a diamond. Using artificial means to mimic a spontaneously occurring natural (or supernatural) phenomenon proves absolutely nothing one way or another.

In this case, Lincoln himself wanted to believe it was merely some optical distortion, some "principle of refraction," and tried very hard to recreate it at-will for others, not only his wife. He was unable to do so. In effect, Lincoln's own "experiment" was a failure.

A close reading of the first-hand accounts of this curious incident points to something other than "optics" as the cause. By his own admission, Lincoln was "well tired out" on November 7th, when he threw himself on his couch at home, so whether due to mental exhaustion or physical fatigue, or simply that by relaxing and allowing his mind to go blank, it is highly likely that Lincoln entered into an altered state of consciousness that produced such a visual effect. Of course, Lincoln's old head injury may well have played a part in this incident as well.

Lincoln, despite his protestations, was clearly disturbed by the experience and that, by itself, is significant. One does not recall a mere trick of a mirror four years later unless it had some special significance. Richard Carpenter claims that the story was already in circulation by the fall of 1864, even though it didn't appear in print until after Lincoln's death.

The First Lady's interpretation on hearing it from her husband was very much in keeping with Lincoln's own previous premonitions of his future fate. Moreover, the fact that the incident happened in close conjunction to his election as president seems more than mere coincidence.

That the incident of the double image actually happened to Lincoln is unquestionable. Whether Lincoln in fact entered into an altered state, wherein he perceived his face as both alive and dead at the same time, is but one interpretation of this uncanny event. However, that this interpretation of Lincoln's encounter eventually proved true is but one more fact in a chain of weird circumstances surrounding the Lincoln presidency.

Regardless of the spin one may put on the incident, there is no arguing with Ward Hill Lamon's description of the incident as "an ominous incident of mysterious character."[49]

Chapter 6

*Inaugural Omens:
Hope and Glory*

"Hurrah for the choice of the nation!
The chieftain so brave and so true;
We'll go for the Great Reformation,
For Lincoln and Liberty too!"

— Hutchinson Family Singers (1860)

Lincoln had won the election of 1860 fairly, but like spoiled children on an old time playground, failing to win by the rules of the game, the slave states — led by South Carolina — left the Union. Lincoln, as President Elect, watched powerless for four long months as one by one the Southern states seceded.

James Buchanan, nominally President for the past four years, chose to do nothing; there were even those who suspected that Buchanan was in collusion with the secessionists. On March 4, 1861, when Abraham Lincoln finally walked onto the platform before the central portico of the Capitol building to be sworn-in, he was a man beset by seemingly insurmountable obstacles.

Before Lincoln stood a crowd of 30,000 on that bright, clear March day to watch him take the oath of office and hear him speak.

Shortly before, however, it looked as though no one would hear him speak. The Capitol Building had been undergoing a major reconstruction, with bits and pieces of stone and steel strewn about the ground. Workmen were scurrying to and fro, busily at work on the scaffolding above. Up until the very last moment before the Inauguration, the workers were busy hammering and sawing, working on the Capitol Dome.

Up until that day, Lincoln had been so absorbed with political affairs and drafting his speech that it had slipped his mind that the building was under construction. He surveyed the building behind and the men engaged in rebuilding, quietly gazing, apparently deep in thought.

To those closest to him, Lincoln remarked that he was glad that the laborers were still busy at work. He commented, "I take it as a sign... So long as work continues on the Capitol, the Union will also continue."[50]

On taking the oath of office, Lincoln proceeded to deliver his Inaugural address. For the most part, the speech was legalistic in tone, attempting to allay fears of the slave states of their right to enslave others. He also made a closing argument for the illegality of secession. Speaking that day was Lincoln the lawyer, not Lincoln the prophet.

However, towards the end of his address, in calling for unity and conciliation, Lincoln allowed himself a moment to talk about the "mystic chords of memory," which joined the nation's dead with its present population. He also expressed the hope — vain as it turned out — that all would somehow join the "chorus of Union," together "touched...by the better angels of our nature."[51]

Lincoln's closing remarks, waxing both poetic and mystical, were oddly out of place with the legalistic body of the speech. It has been theorized that his Secretary of State, Seward, was the one who suggested the "better angels" passage. Whether it was Seward or Lincoln, clearly towards the end, the "better angels" did speak to him.

Four years later, on that same day, Lincoln experienced another sign — as did all those present for the inauguration.

By March 1865, the Capitol building's dome was finished, but the war was not. The fall election crisis had

Lincoln's First Inauguration, March 4, 1861. The Capitol was still under reconstruction at the time; Lincoln viewed the work behind him as an omen that the United States would also be rebuilt and made whole once more.

passed, however; the people had elected to let Lincoln finish his task and all talk of a negotiated "peace" — capitulation to secessionism — was dead. The Confederacy was now but an empty shell, ready to collapse at any time.

If prospects for the future finally seemed bright for the nation, Inauguration Day was not. The day was a gloomy one, with clouds hanging grey and low over the ceremony. Shortly after noon, the President rose from his seat. A roar of applause welled up from the crowd, flowing and ebbing "like sweeping waves upon the shore."

Just as Lincoln made ready to speak, the threatening clouds suddenly spread apart. It was as if the clouds were heavenly curtains, parting on some divine stage. A brilliant burst of light came forth from the opening above, the beam of light bathing the President in a luminous aura "and flooded the spectacle with glory."[52] The incident made a deep impression on all present, not least upon the President.

To a journalist attending the ceremony, Lincoln later remarked, "Did you notice that sunburst? It made my heart jump." Lincoln then confessed, "I am just superstitious enough to consider it a happy omen."[53]

Lincoln's Second Inauguration,
March 4, 1865.

Later, in his note accompanying the bible on which Lincoln took his oath of office, Salmon P. Chase, now Chief Justice of the Supreme Court, comments to the First Lady about the sunburst as "an auspicious omen of the dispersion of the clouds of war and the restoration of the clear sunlight of prosperous peace."[54]

Viewed from the distance of a century and a half, neither Lincoln's First Inaugural sign nor his Second Inaugural omen may seem to the modern skeptic of much import. At the very least, however, they are both indicative of Lincoln's state of mind. At those two momentous points in time, even as Lincoln assumed the mantle of power, he could not help but see affirmations of his pre-ordained mission in the environment around him.

So long as man has gazed up to the skies or looked about him on earth, he has seen pointers to a greater reality that lies beneath the surface of daily existence. Sometimes they are but affirmations of one's existing path; at other times they advise of future events, be they for good or ill. These are called signs and omens respectively.

For the ancient kings of Assyria, to find a locust sitting on the throne was an omen of the worst sort, for it meant a threat to the realm. The Old Testament is filled with "signs and wonders" and we know that while he was not a "technical Christian," Lincoln certainly knew his King James.

Lincoln's Second Inaugural in particular is laden with biblical imagery; indeed, he interprets the whole war in terms of God's divine judgment. The reporter for a British newspaper described the speech as "something of a sacred and almost prophetic character."[55] While most biographers have emphasized the conciliatory passages of the Second Inaugural, a close reading of the document indicates that Lincoln was thinking more of God's divine wrath — a wrath that had spared neither side.

"Woe unto the world because of offenses....woe to that man by whom offences cometh!" Lincoln tells the crowd. The President then tells them: "If we shall suppose that American Slavery is one of those offences...He now wills to remove and that He gives to both North and South this terrible war."

Although Lincoln does pray "that this mighty scourge of war may speedily pass away," he also enjoins his listeners that "if God wills that it continue, until all the wealth piled by the bond-man's two hundred and fifty years of unrequited toil shall be sunk, and until every drop of blood drawn with the lash shall be paid by another drawn with the sword...the judgments of the Lord are true and righteous."[56]

Clearly, by March of 1865, Lincoln saw in the war more of God's "terrible swift sword" and the fulfillment of a foreordained divine destiny. However, if the end of the war was the fulfillment of this divine destiny, then Lincoln's mission, too, was coming to an end — and the completion of his own personal destiny — a destiny he had foreseen since early youth.

Lincoln's Second Inauguration, March 4, 1865. In the midst of the ceremony, as Lincoln was about to deliver his address, a brilliant beam of light broke through the gloom and shone on Lincoln as he began his speech. Lincoln and many of those present took it as a divine omen.

Chapter 7

The Phantom Cannon

At what point, then, is the approach of danger to be expected?
I answer, if it ever reach us it must spring up amongst us.

— *Abraham Lincoln (1838)*

Southern secessionists moved swiftly to separate their states from the Union. Not just in Charleston, but throughout the South, arsenals and forts were seized by radicals — often before their states had even voted to secede. The small Federal army, broadly scattered from coast to coast, was too weak to resist; some army officers, moreover, aided and abetted the secessionist seizures.

For several weeks following the inauguration, Washington, D.C. became more and more isolated. The Capitol was virtually defenseless and it seemed that every day that passed the situation became more critical, especially since it wasn't until April 18th that the first loyal troops began to trickle into the Capitol. However, with the attack and surrender of Fort Sumter just four days before, the political situation worsened considerably. Several more states joined the rebellion, including Virginia.

Even in those slave states that did not secede, the situation was tenuous, with Rebel sympathizers turning violent and trying their best to drag their "neutral" states in the fray. On April 19th, for example, Southern militants in Baltimore cut the telegraph lines and bridges leading to Washington; then a mob attacked a Massachusetts regiment as it was marching from one train station to another — soldiers and rioters alike died in the mêlée.

Towards the end of April, one of the many visitors to the White House was the German-American politician Carl Schurz. He had come from Wisconsin to offer help in rallying German immigrants to the cause. Schurz even offered to organize a "Prussian" cavalry regiment, although, ironically, it was not that many years before as a fiery young revolutionary in Germany that he had spent some time avoiding the blades of Prussian cavalry. During the course of Schurz's discussions with Lincoln, the President confided in him about an uncanny incident that had taken place only a short time before.

One afternoon, shortly after issuing the call on April 14th for 75,000 volunteers to defend the Union, Lincoln was sitting alone in his office at the White House when, suddenly, a feeling came over him "as if he were utterly deserted and helpless."

Lincoln's melancholy in this case was well justified, as he later told Schurz, "Any moderately strong body of Secessionist troops, if there were any in the neighborhood, might (have) come over the Long Bridge across the Potomac and just take me and the members of the cabinet — the whole lot of them."[57]

Even as Lincoln meditates on this unhappy scenario, he suddenly hears what sounds like a booming cannon. The President said to himself: "There they are!"

At any moment, Lincoln fully expected someone to rush in with news of an attack on the city. When no one comes with news of battle, Lincoln asks his White House staff if they have heard the cannon's report, but no one but he heard the loud sound.

When no news of battle arrives at the White House, Lincoln resolves to investigate the cause of the mysterious cannonade. Is the Capitol being caught off-guard? Lincoln can stand to wait no longer; he leaves the White House to find out.

Lincoln goes out onto the street and begins walking. He walks and walks and walks, his long, loping gate making rapid progress along the boulevard. All is still. Where is the report of battle? Where is the shouting and din of men in arms?

Lincoln finally comes to the Federal Arsenal. Going up to the entrance, he finds it completely unguarded. The doors to the arsenal are wide open with no one in sight. "Anybody might have gone and helped himself to the arms," Lincoln tells Schurz several days later. Lincoln himself secures the storehouse of munitions and arms.

Lincoln's return journey to the White House is free of disturbance. Nonetheless, the incident is unsettling for the President. While his fear of a surprise attack was unfounded, his intuition of danger was quite real. Failing to secure the Federal supply of military stores, any and all who wished harm to the government would be free to pillage the city.

Afterwards, despite making a thorough canvas, the President confirms that no one else heard the mysterious phantom cannon alerting him that night of danger. Was the phantom cannon merely an auditory hallucination on the part of Lincoln? Given the President's state of mind, his grave concern for the capitol, its lack of defenses, and its want of a garrison, it could be a possibility... but what of the unguarded arsenal? If Lincoln's concerns about the cannon's roar had proven unfounded, one could easily dismiss the incident as a case of the jitters; however, the arsenal was open and it was unguarded — the danger was quite real. The President's prescience had prevented a dangerous threat to the Capitol.

Then, as later in the war, there were many secessionists in the city only too willing to do harm to the United Sates government and its leaders. An arsenal of explosives, powder, shot, cannon, muskets, and other weapons left wide open so that "anybody might have gone in and helped himself to the arms" was a potential Pandora's box of trouble.[58]

Lincoln was deep in meditation at the time, contemplating the looming dangers that were besetting the capitol. That Lincoln should suddenly be made aware of such a danger at that particular moment seems more than mere chance. The incident, as related by a loyal confidante of the administration, has all the earmarks of a spontaneous psychic warning arising from deep within the mysterious mind of Lincoln. Call it sixth sense, second sight, or a presentiment...whatever label one may choose to attach to the incident, surely Abraham Lincoln had it in abundance.

Chapter 8

Protect the Flag!

*"I believe in my conscience that it is a duty we
owe ourselves and our children, and our God, to protect this
Government and that flag from every assailant, be he who he may."*
— Stephen Douglas, April 25, 1861

Flag Raising ceremony. Although most attending were not aware of the ill omen that occurred, both the President and those close to him were deeply affected.

There is an aura that surrounds certain flags, which transcends their mere material existence. In his last public speech before his death, Stephen Douglas' final thoughts were of protecting the flag and the nation for which it stood. Men have fought and died over such pieces of cloth. During the Civil War, it was deemed an honor to be the color bearer of a regiment — an honor that generally proved fatal. Certainly, to desecrate a nation's flag is tantamount to an act of war. Similarly, flag ceremonies are always fraught with rituals that bespeak of almost religious devotion, all the more so in times of war. With the *Stars and Stripes*, the aura surrounding the flag goes beyond patriotic symbolism to an almost mystical veneration.[59]

When the Southern states began to secede, one of the first acts of the Rebels was to tear down the American flag and replace it with the "Bonnie Blue Flag." Before there was a Confederacy, or even a Confederate flag, this banner — a single white star on a field of blue — was the symbol of secessionism.

This "Lone Star" flag actually goes back long before the war. In 1810, a group of wild frontiersmen proclaimed the "Republic of West Florida," which at the time was part of Spanish territory. Later, in the 1830s, as Americans began filtering into northern Mexico, they rebelled and proclaimed the "Republic of Texas," also adopting the "Bonnie Blue Flag." Thus, in 1861, as the slave states separated one by one, this "lone star" flag became the natural symbol of the Secessionists.

Some disgusted Union politicians suggested to Lincoln that he should have the secession states' stars removed from the national flag. Lincoln would have none of it: the Union was one and indivisible. As long as Lincoln was president, the American flag, like the Union, would be one and indivisible.

Therefore, by June 1861, with the Secession Crisis rapidly descending into an all-out war, the replacement ceremony of the old American flag on the White House grounds took on an intense new significance.

The official retirement of the US flag at the White House has always been a portentous ritual, but now it was especially so with war virtually lapping at the Capitol's door. On June 29th, a large crowd gathered on the south lawn of the White House to watch the President raise the new flag.

That same morning, Lincoln held a cabinet meeting, inviting his chief military leaders to hold forth on what policy to pursue should peaceful methods of reconciliation finally fail. General Winfield Scott pushed for an expedition down the Mississippi combined with a naval blockade — the so-called Anaconda Plan. General Irwin McDowell presented his plan to attack the Confederate forces gather under General Beauregard near Manassas, Virginia: a quick blow against the Rebel army and they will all flee, he argued. Some cabinet members argued for delay, saying that the new Union army was too green; Lincoln, though, pointed out that the Confederate troops were also green.

After the serious morning meeting, it was hoped the flag ceremony would prove a pleasant diversion. Mrs. Lincoln was already on the South Portico, where Mrs. Taft and her daughter Julia had arrived to join her. The President arrived with generals and their aides in tow, as well as members of the cabinet. A cluster of society ladies festooned in broad hoop skirts and blossoming bonnets cackled to one side while at the center of the gathering stood the President. His tall spare frame was distinctive and set him apart at the base of the flagpole.

At the appointed time, the Marine Band began playing the *Star Spangled Banner*. All arise, army officers at attention saluting while male civilians remove their hats. When the President's large hands pull on the halyard to raise the new flag, however, the cord jams.

A youth filled with hard manual labor has given Lincoln a great deal of physical strength; the rail-splitter from Illinois yanked on the rope harder, trying to force the Stars and Stripes to do his bidding and ascend to its full height. Instead of yielding to the President's full strength, the upper corner of the flag tears off and hangs down. There it stands, still flying but with a group of the stars torn away and hanging, separated from the main body of the other stars.

A young Julia Taft noted at the time, "A gasp of surprise and horror at the sinister omen went around." It was at this point that a young staff officer near at hand has the presence of mind to step up to a group of ladies clustered nearby and under his breath hiss, "Pins! Pins!"

In those days, elegantly dressed ladies had an abundance of pins in their clothes, so the ladies donated their spare fasteners for the cause. Julia's mother herself volunteered several, as did Mrs. Lincoln,[60] and the army repaired the rent in the flag, which happened to coincide with the exact number of seceded states. The flag, restored to unity, was now raised to full mast without further ado.

A bit further away from the flagpole, Benjamin French, a Lincoln appointee, had also noticed the rip and he, too, took it as an omen of ill fortune. "My only consolation," he noted, "was observing the determined energy with which the President pulled away at the halyard...let what reverse may come he will meet them...and bring us out of the war, if with a tattered flag, still all will be there!"[61]

The general public out on the South Lawn was unaware of the ill omen or its final resolution. The Marine Band continued to play until the flag rose up the flagpole while the artillery boomed a salute and the crowd cheered. Aside from the brief delay, the average onlooker had no inkling of anything amiss.

A reporter, N. P. Willis, also was unaware of the ill omen. However, he did note that on the President's face "a curious problem of expression." To the reporter, Lincoln "seemed withdrawn into an inner sanctuary of thought, feeling the scene's far reach into the future."[62]

Julia Taft's father took the incident seriously and commented to her that news of what really happened would be suppressed, lest it hurt enlistments. She tells us that of the senior officers present, General Banks was much disturbed by the omen. Mr. Taft, commenting in his diary, wrote that he hoped the general "will keep his discomposure to himself."[63]

Julia informs us that Lincoln "felt a sharper pang than any of us," but that "with his mystic nature there was a strange combination of hard common sense" as well and that doubtless he, too, would soon put the ill omen out of mind.[64]

It would be years after the war before reports of the omen would see the light of day. In hindsight, it perhaps seemed a minor disturbance; yet for those who witnessed it, it was clear that President Lincoln and the members of his administration present took the ill omen quite seriously.

Was the sundering of the Stars and Stripes mere chance? With every little aspect of the American flag and the flag-raising heavily laden with symbolism, it seemed far more than mere coincidence to Lincoln and his team. Occurring at a time of growing crisis, with the President and his administration facing new challenges almost daily, an ominous incident pointing to even greater danger was not a sign of the time anyone in the government wished to see.

Chapter 9

Star of the North: The War Comet

"Before the War I saw the elements all red as blood and I saw after that a great comet; and they said there was going to be a war."[65]

— *Frank A. Patterson, former slave*

STAR OF THE NORTH, OR THE COMET OF 1861.

The War Comet. Appearing soon after the beginning of the war, Thatcher's Comet was widely regarded as a harbinger of war by people North and South — Lincoln included. This piece of war propaganda portrays President Lincoln as the comet, rapidly descending on the rebellious states.

Of all the omens and portents known to humanity throughout the ages, surely the most dire of them all is the appearance in the heavens of a Great Comet. The arrival of such a celestial event inevitably presages famine, death, and war.

It is on this account that the Chinese refer to the comet as a "broom-star," for it sweeps all before it. Indeed, our own English word "disaster" actually refers to the comet as well, literally meaning "bad star" (dis-astra).

Sun, moon, and stars have all been consulted to guide men's destinies: to predict peace and war, planting and harvesting, fair weather and foul, and all manner of other human endeavors. Only the comet has consistently been taken as a malign sign.

When Hannibal saw a comet, he took it as an omen of his final defeat and committed suicide. Julius Caesar's assassination was associated with the appearance of a comet. Nero began murdering his political opponents and Christians at the appearance of such a "hairy star."

The advent of Christianity did nothing to allay people's fears about such heavenly omens. Constantine the Great, the first Christian emperor, died soon after the appearance of a comet in the skies. One Pope went so far as to excommunicate a comet that appeared at the time that Constantinople fell to the Turks. So far as is known, the comet did not repent and ask the Pope's forgiveness.[66]

Even as the United States of America was hurtling towards a disintegrated union, from the inky depth of space came forth yet another "bad star." Though sighted in the Southern hemisphere first, in Australia, on May 13, 1861, the comet became visible in the Northern hemisphere around the end of June. It came to be known as the War Comet.[67]

North and South, word spread of the ominous portent. Given the state of the Union at the time, the celestial wanderer was widely observed and commented on.

In the mountains and valleys where North Carolina meets Tennessee there lived at the time a legendary Wise Woman — some called her a witch — by the name of Granny Weiss. One popular account, committed to paper generations later, says she went into a trance "and spelled up the whole dang war." Oral tradition relates how "she seen a star from the north sky travel clear across the heaven and run smack dab into a star in the south end of the sky."[68]

Union propaganda seized on the comet as a portent that meant the imminent suppression of the rebellion. One image, printed on patriotic envelopes, depicts Lincoln as the "Star of the North" hurtling through the sky like a comet. Another piece of popular propaganda similarly shows General Winfield Scott descending from the heavens with the caption: "About this time you will hear thunder."[69]

Abraham Lincoln's own association with comets actually goes back several years before the appearance of the War Comet. In 1858, another Great Comet had made its appearance in the skies over the nation. Called Donati's Comet (C/1858 L1), it, too, was widely regarded as a harbinger of ill tidings. Secession had not yet become a reality, but already politicians were hotly debating the issue of slavery. The war of words had already begun; the shooting war was still three years away.

On September 14, 1858, the day before the third of the Lincoln-Douglas debates, Abe did not spend it preparing for his verbal duel on the morrow. Rather, the Rail-Splitter spent it in the company of a reporter from Chicago gazing up at the night sky. According to Horace White of the *Chicago Press and Tribune*, the two men sat on the porch of Lincoln's hotel staring at the comet. "Mr. Lincoln greatly admired the strange visitor," White tells us, "and he and I sat for an hour or more in front of the hotel looking at it."[70]

Elsewhere in Illinois, at least one prairie preacher was exhorting his listeners that the comet was a divine sign. At a back-country revival, he told his congregation, "The Lord...

he hez opened the roof o' Heaven so ye can all see what's a-comin'.... Under ye the stars air begin te shift en wonder. A besom o' destruction il overtake them that's on the wrong side in this here fight."

The preacher concluded his homespun homily with a prophecy: "He shall send them a saviour, en a great one, en he shell deliver them... ask yerselves who it air that's a-cryin for deliverance...Why thar ain't but one people a-cryin for deliverance, an they are slaves down thar in Egypt!"[71]

In 1858, Lincoln was only just beginning to emerge on the national scene, but the advent of Doneti's Comet made many connect it to the great issues of the day. The preacher's prophecy was made not knowing of Honest Abe's own date with destiny.

While Lincoln's own thoughts as to this comet have not been recorded, he was clearly intensely interested in the heavenly portent.

By July 1861, the backcountry preacher's prophecy seemed close to coming true. The Southern states were already in an active state of rebellion and both sides were busy arming themselves. A major outbreak could happen at any time. All-out war seemed inevitable.

In Washington, Lincoln's government seemed isolated from the rest of the country; Virginia was now firmly in the Rebel camp while Maryland, too, seemed to teeter on the edge of secession. If Maryland fell, the Capitol would be completely cut off. Even within the city of Washington, its residents were of dubious loyalty. General Winfield Scott had made sure when Lincoln was inaugurated that sharpshooters were on every roof and a battery of artillery was placed to guard the President's route to the inauguration.

One person who was privy to the happenings within the White House at this time was Julia Taft. She was the daughter of Horatio Taft, a government official who was a "War Democrat," loyal to Lincoln and the Union's cause. Julia's two younger brothers were about the same age as the two youngest Lincoln boys and the Taft children were often invited to the White House to play.

Mrs. Lincoln never had daughters of her own and the teenage Julia soon became a favorite of the First Lady. Julia's memoirs of her visits to the White House form a unique chronicle of incidents that never made it into the "official" biographies; this was especially true of certain uncanny incidents and openly expressed paranormal beliefs relating to the Lincoln White House.

Julia Taft also took note of the War Comet's arrival. She observed that "while fear of an attack thus held the city in its grasp, the Negroes cowered under the great War Comet blazing in the sky." It so happened that a neighbor of the Tafts, a family named Woodward, owned an old slave named Oola, "said to be a native African," who held forth to Julia about the comet.

Oola was tall and sturdy of frame, her skin grayish black and as wrinkled as a raisin's. On the top of her head, tufts of white wool blossomed all over. It was her eyes,

President Lincoln and son Tad. Reflecting their father's belief in the paranormal, Tad and his brother Willie often informed their father of reported signs or omens, such as the War Comet and the African American seer Oola's prophecy about it.

however, that were Oola's most distinguishing feature. Her eyes would flash with a sudden glare that sent chills through whoever they were aimed at, including Julia. The other servants of the neighborhood held her in awe — and not a little fear — and believed she had the evil eye and could "conjure spells."

Even as the War Comet blazed in the night sky, Julia and her brothers dared to have their fortune told by Oola. Julia tells us it was "a terrifying yet fascinating experience." Julia — and the Lincolns — got more than they expected from Oola.

"Dat's a great war comin and de handle's to'rd de Norf and de point to'rd de Souf and de Norf's gwine take dat sword and cut de Souf's heart out," Oola informed them. However, Oola added, "dat Linkum man, chilluns, if he takes de sword, he's gwine perish by it."[72]

Julia and her brothers told the Lincoln boys about Oola's prophecy regarding the War Comet, but carefully omitted the part about the President's death. Tad, in particular, was greatly impressed by Oola's sooth-saying and ran straight to his father to convey her words.

Julia was present when Tad told his parents about the prophecy. Mrs. Lincoln laughed off the tale, but the President "seemed strangely impressed." Lincoln, in fact, asked Tad to repeat Oola's prophecy, which the boy eagerly did.

After the second recital, Tad said, "Do you think that's what it means, Pa?"

"I hope not, Tad," answered Lincoln in a serious tone. "I hope it won't come to that."

A few evenings later, Julia Taft was back at the White House. She saw the President looking out the window, staring up at the comet intently. He was apparently still mulling over the old prophet's words; however, Oola was not the only African American prophet who read the signs rightly.

At the outset, we quoted one former slave to the same effect. Later in the war, a white school marm working with freedmen down at Hilton Head, South Carolina, relayed a similar message from a 53-year-old former slave named George Washington. At the time, George was expressing his gratitude, but he related how when he was seventeen years old he had a prophetic dream: "I saw a comet come from the North to the South and I said good Lord what is that? I heard a voice, 'There shall be wars and rumors of wars,' and I saw many signs and wonders."[73]

There were signs and wonders upon the Pharaoh, too, before the Israelites were freed from bondage.

Of course, Lincoln did not need any prophet or prophetess to tell him what the War Comet meant. War and death, whether his own or others, were on the lips of many who gazed up in the sky that July. Oola's prophecy merely confirmed something Lincoln was already only too aware of.

At the time Julia Taft related Oola's prophecy to the Lincolns, there still remained a glimmer of hope that somehow the administration might solve the Secession crisis without serious bloodshed. Only a few weeks later, that last hope was dashed.

On July 21, 1861, Union and Confederate forces clashed at Manassas Junction, Virginia. The Battle of Bull Run, as the North named it, was a serious defeat for the Union. It meant no quick resolution of the crisis; war — real war — had arrived. In the wake of the fiasco, there were many in the North who looked to the skies and cried that the War Comet had foretold the defeat. Indeed, who could blame them?

In the end, however, it was Oola's interpretation of the bad star's appearance that proved the correct one. The South was defeated — and it did cost Lincoln his life. We know that Lincoln loved both the King James Bible and William Shakespeare for the beauty of their language. Perhaps, as he gazed up at that malevolent star in July 1861, he may have mused on Shakespere's lines from *Julius Caesar*: "When beggars die there are no comets seen; the heavens themselves blaze forth the death of princes."

Chapter 10

Thenceforward & Forever: The Emancipation Sign

God had decided this question in favor of the slaves.

— *Abraham Lincoln*

When Abraham Lincoln ran for president in 1860, and even well after he was in office and fighting to preserve the Union, he was at pains to repeatedly emphasize to the public that he had no plans to abolish slavery. Throughout the early phases of the war, Lincoln resisted pressure from Northern Abolitionists and the Radical Republicans in Congress to do so. Honest Abe even publicly reprimanded Federal commanders who openly recruited African Americans as soldiers or welcomed runaways into territory occupied by Union troops.

Lincoln was morally opposed to the institution of slavery, but at the outset of the war he was not an abolitionist. Before the war Abe had condemned John Brown and his followers, as well as anyone who advocated violence to end slavery. Contrary to the rabid propaganda of the Secessionists and their Copperhead sympathizers up North, Lincoln had tried very hard to steer a moderate path between the two political extremes. Truth be told, at the beginning of the war, the number of those folks in the North actually willing to go to war to end slavery was very small — and Lincoln knew it.

However, as the war dragged on and the battles became bloodier and public attitudes more bitter, Lincoln, as well as many others in the North, began to change his attitude on the issue of freeing the slaves. Union soldiers at the front were not inclined to return runaway slaves to the very masters who were in rebellion and trying to kill them. Very vocal radicals in Congress and in the press also clamored for action on the slave issue. Moreover, great men like Frederick Douglass began to educate and inform Lincoln more deeply on the issues involved, including the use of slaves as a powerful weapon against the South.[74]

Therefore, by the summer of 1862, Lincoln had come to see that by attacking slavery he would also have a powerful tool with which to save the Union. Typical of Lincoln, this point of view was at once both idealistic and eminently practical at the same time.

In finally coming to this decision to emancipate the slaves of the Confederacy, Lincoln expressed the belief that it was not he but fate that had forced his hand in the matter. Writing to a political ally, Lincoln said, "I claim not to have controlled events, but confess plainly that events have controlled me."[75]

Similarly, in 1866, Joseph Gillespie, one of Lincoln's friends and pre-war legal associates, affirmed that "after he became President he gave unmistakable indications of being a believer in destiny.... Mr. Lincoln had strong a faith that it was the purposes of the Almighty to save this country as ever Moses had that God would deliver the Israelites from bondage, and he came to believe that he himself was an instrument foreordained to aid in the accomplishment of this purpose as well as to emancipate the slaves."[76]

In late July 1862, Lincoln presented a draft of the Emancipation Proclamation to his cabinet. Only one member opposed the idea outright, although several cabinet members offered suggestions to improve or strengthen it. Secretary of State

Lincoln signing the preliminary Emancipation Proclamation, September 1862; original painting by Frank Carpenter. At the time of this meeting, Lincoln confessed to his cabinet that he had held off issuing the proclamation until he received a divine sign.

Seward, however, raised objections as to the timing and suggested the President delay it, to await a time more favorable to the cause, where it would appear to be issued from a position of strength and not one of weakness.

In the end, Lincoln concurred with Seward and the proclamation was postponed. As Lincoln explained later, he resolved to wait for a sign that would let him know that the time was right to issue the decree.

Lincoln was facing mounting pressure from the Abolitionist press to end slavery at once. Still, Lincoln kept the draft of the decree in his desk drawer, waiting for his hoped for sign. Meanwhile, those inside the administration in favor of emancipation feared that Lincoln would succumb to pressure from the opposite quarter, from those opposed to freeing the slaves, and renege on his proposal.

William Lloyd Garrison, the fiery Abolitionist publisher, called Lincoln "nothing better than a wet rag." Frederick Douglas said that Lincoln was allowing himself to be a tool of "traitors and rebels" while Horace Greeley urged Republican politicians to give the President hell until he fell in line with their radical agenda.

Despite mounting pressure, Lincoln continued to prosecute the war as before and await a sign that would tell him the time was right. Unfortunately, with General McClellan in command of the mighty Army of the Potomac, there was a very real possibility that any such sign of divine favor would never appear.

Appointed commander of the army after the debacle at Bull Run, McClellan had re-organized and trained the Army of the Potomac into a first-class fighting unit. However, whatever virtues McClellan possessed in the area of organization or on the drilling ground, he totally lacked when on the field of battle.

In truth, McClellan was so concerned about not losing a battle that he seemed incapable of winning one. Time after time, Little Mac's timidity in combat had cost the Union a chance at victory. Nor was this "War Democrat" at all in favor of freeing the slaves — still less using them as soldiers.

So, when General Lee and the Army of Northern Virginia crossed the Potomac in September 1862, beginning an invasion of the North, the fact that McClellan was charged with defeating the Rebels onslaught did not bode well for Lincoln's hoped for sign. Quite the contrary, the situation seemed quite dire. Not only might Lee threaten Washington with capture, the slave-state of Maryland, still in the Union, was expected to declare for the Confederacy at any time. On the other side of the Atlantic, moreover, one more Union defeat might cause Great Britain and France to recognize the Confederacy as a sovereign nation; if they did, then untold military and economic resources might be put at the Rebels' disposal.

Even as things seemed blackest for Lincoln and liberty, a curious thing occurred. Out of the blue, two Federal couriers stumbled across a bundle of cigars, wrapped in a sheath of papers. The bundle had been lying in open sight along their path, almost as if put there on purpose. At first, the soldiers were more interested in the cigars — a heavenly windfall for any Yankee soldier — and paid little heed to their covering.

Slowly unrolling the sheets to gain access to the treasure within, it gradually dawned on the soldiers that those seemingly worthless papers were no less than General Robert E. Lee's complete plan of war for the invasion of Maryland, down to the most minute detail!

Even historians have described the discovery of these documents as nothing less than a god-send. To this day no one knows how those papers came to be lying in that field. Historians still regard their sudden appearance in Federal hands as a mystery.

However, despite the seemingly miraculous turn in events, another miracle still needed to happen: to get General McClellan to actually take action and win a battle. It almost didn't happen.

They say that McClellan was an excellent judge of good horse flesh. One wonders how this could be true since now, as on previous occasions, he insisted on looking a gift horse in the mouth.

Although the administration was elated at the windfall, McClellan was reluctant to make use of the information that had fallen into his lap undeserved. At first suspecting a ruse, when Little Mac did finally

Lincoln meeting with General McClellan after the Battle of Antietam. The President interpreted the Union's victory as an omen that the time was right to issue his proclamation freeing the slaves. However, getting McClellan to fight any battle with the enemy was a miracle in itself.

move, it was with great caution. A bolder general would have moved aggressively to cut off General Lee, destroy his army piecemeal, and thereby end the war. Not Little Mac.

Regardless, McClellan did finally move and met Lee near the town of Sharpsburg, Maryland, and there fought the Grey Fox to a standstill. It was the bloodiest single-day in American history.

When the smoke had cleared, Lee was in retreat back to Virginia. McClellan was left with an empty battlefield full of dead and dying and little inclination to follow Lee. Nonetheless, the North could — and did — claim victory.

While historians have generally described the Battle of Antietam as a draw, with neither side obtaining a clear victory, Lincoln saw the matter differently. Abe Lincoln the frontiersman looked upon Civil War battles in much the same light as he used to view a backwoods brawl: the last man standing claimed victory. So long as the Union Army was in possession of the battlefield at the end and the enemy was withdrawing — well, that was victory fair and square in Abe's view.

Strategically, Lee's planned invasion of Maryland had failed to achieve its goals; moreover, overseas the perception that the North had won prevailed. Lincoln at last had his divine sign.

Only five days after Antietam, on September 22, 1862, Lincoln called a cabinet meeting at which he formally announced his decision to issue the Emancipation Proclamation. At this meeting, Lincoln openly remarked to his cabinet that since their last discussion of this issue, he "had made a vow, a covenant."

Apparently, shortly before Antietam, Lincoln explained, he had made a sacred vow "that if God gave us the victory in the approaching battle, he would consider it an indication of Divine will... that it was his duty to move forward in the cause of emancipation." Almost apologetically, Lincoln confessed that "it might be thought strange...that he had in this way submitted the disposal of matters when the way was not clear," even in his own mind.[77]

In the end, Lincoln was satisfied that he had been right to leave the final decision to Providence. Lincoln truly believed that it was his vow to God that had caused the victory. One thing is sure: it certainly wasn't McClellan's generalship. As Lincoln himself put it, "God had decided this question in favor of the slaves."[78]

Many dismissed Lincoln's sentiments at this meeting, as well as similar expressions of his fatalism, as mere political rhetoric. They were uttered, it is said, for popular consumption. Yet if we look at Lincoln's long-standing belief in his own destiny — that he was fated to lead the country in this its hour of peril — it's hard to avoid the conclusion that Lincoln meant what he said literally.

Chapter 11

Lincoln and Destiny

"I cannot avoid believing in predestination."

— *Abraham Lincoln*

On the face of it, it may seem odd that the President of the United States should surrender a decision so momentous as the issuing of the Emancipation Declaration to the whims of chance, much less believe that Providence was speaking directly to him. Yet the Emancipation Sign was but one of several documented cases where Lincoln did indeed leave the course of events to the invisible hand of destiny.

We have seen how in his youth Lincoln held firm to the belief that destiny had something great in store for him. As Abe grew and matured, this vision of glory, this belief in his own personal destiny, became clearer and more specific.

Mainstream historians have traditionally been divided on this point. There are those scholars who accept that Lincoln possessed a fatalistic streak, even if they see a sociological cause for it, but there are many who have dismissed this core belief of Lincoln's as either mere political rhetoric or as neurosis — or even as something later attributed to him after death by his many eulogizers.[79] It behooves us, therefore, to take a closer look at Lincoln's notion of having a preordained destiny and the context in which this belief existed since it is so closely tied to all his other paranormal experiences.

If we piece-meal this, it is easy to dismiss Lincoln's fatalism. In isolation, his different statements on the subject can be rationalized and explained away. Taken as a whole, however, it is clear the Lincoln sincerely held to the notion of a personal destiny and that

he came to believe that his was closely tied to the fate of the nation.

Of course, in trying to make sense of Lincoln's many comments on the subject, it doesn't help that Lincoln himself was often of two minds on the subject. For example, when Lincoln told fellow lawyer Joseph Gillespie that he could not avoid believing in predestination, he then followed it up by also saying that it was a "very unprofitable field of speculation." Lincoln confessed to his lawyer friend that "it was hard to reconcile that belief with responsibility for one's acts."[80]

Nonetheless, his longtime friend and law partner, William Herndon, averred that Lincoln "held most firmly to the doctrine of fatalism all his life."[81] Similarly, Mary Todd Lincoln tells us in no uncertain terms that her husband's "only philosophy was, what is to be will be, and no prayers of ours can reverse the decree."[82]

In the 1850s, Lincoln expressed to a fellow politician, Orville Browning, that he was certain that he had in store "some important predestined labor or work." Lincoln was later more specific, saying during the war that he "was an instrument foreordained to aid in the accomplishment of this purpose (putting down the rebellion) as well as to emancipate the slaves."[83]

In these and other conversations with those close to him, Lincoln frequently used several different phrases to describe this long-standing belief: Fate or fatalism, predestination, destiny, preordained, and the like. In reporting these conversations, Lincoln's friends and supporters often used the terms interchangeably, although the words don't necessarily all have the same precise meaning.

The one term most commonly commented on by scholars was that of predestination. The term is deeply rooted in Protestant theology, although during the nineteenth century it came more and more to have a secular, non-religious connotation.

Once Martin Luther had broken the Papal monopoly in Christian doctrine, other thinkers quickly arose, preaching their own doctrines and interpretations of the Bible. Notable among them was John Calvin, the Scots religious leader. Taking the lead from a Swiss Protestant theologian, he developed the Doctrine of Predestination, which held that God had foreordained who would be saved and who would go to Hell. Those few whom God had chosen for heaven were the "elect."

This strain of Protestant theology soon proved popular among the Scots and Scots-Irish, but also spread throughout the rest of the British Isles, with the Puritans also adopting the doctrine. Regarding this particular version of predestination, Abe himself quoted the anecdote about a gentleman from the Carolinas who was asked if it was true that of the whole human race, only persons from one certain congregation in his state would go to heaven. The gentleman allegedly replied, "Yes, sir and damn few of them!"

While predestination originally applied only to spiritual salvation, in America this idea became secularized and spread through society as a whole. It came to be applied at first to one's own personal material fate in life, but then ultimately applied to the destiny of the nation as a whole.

Perhaps the most famous — some would say "infamous" — secular expression of predestination was in the idea of Manifest Destiny. First promoted by a gentleman named O'Connor, it said that the United States was fated to stretch from sea to shining sea. Throughout the nineteenth century, many Americans subscribed to Manifest Destiny wholeheartedly. Ultimately, it came to be a self-fulfilling prophecy.

Lincoln was opposed to the doctrine of Manifest Destiny, because he saw in it the potential for slavery to be extended into new territories to the west. When it came to his own personal destiny, however, Lincoln was unquestionably a believer.

In trying to find the origin of Lincoln's belief that he had a foreordained mission in life — that he was predestined to accomplish some great task — many historians have looked to Lincoln's family background and their Calvinist religious beliefs. It is true that Lincoln's parents were what has been called "hard-shell" Baptists. They were strict adherents to a flavor of Baptist Protestantism that adhered to the original version of predestination. While his parents' theology may have preconditioned the young Abe Lincoln to some extent, it is doubtful that this was the true source of his belief in his own personal destiny.

For one thing, we know that Abe had a rather distant relationship with his father and shared few values in common with him. For another, we have the testimony of his law partner that young Lincoln was, if anything, closer to being an agnostic or even atheist than a "hard-shell" fundamentalist. It is clear that when discussing his fatalism to friends and associates, Lincoln is referring to his role on earth. His role is somehow foreordained, that much Lincoln is certain of; by whom or what remained unclear, at least in his early years. Certainly, it had little to do with Calvinism.

This is not to say that Lincoln did not try to rationalize his fatalism in some fashion. Here Lincoln's skepticism and doubts about religion were clearly at war with his belief that some unseen power was at work in his life, leading him inexorably to an already determined fate. In his young adulthood, he developed what he called the "Doctrine of Necessity," in which he tried to explain in a non-theological way how all human behavior was predetermined. However, as one reads Lincoln's reasoning behind this doctrine, where motive and self-interest are made the well-springs of a kind of humanistic determinism, his reasoning seems rooted more in legal theory than in either theology or metaphysics.[84]

Lincoln's "Doctrine of Necessity" seems to be less a logical explanation of his beliefs than his attempt to rationalize a deeply rooted belief that he already held, one that essentially defied all reason. Throughout this period, Lincoln the religious skeptic was very much at war with Lincoln the mystic.

As Lincoln's career drew him ever more deeply into the issues of slavery and secession, so, too, did his spiritual beliefs seem to be drawn ever more closer to his innate mysticism. More and more, Lincoln uses the word "God" and less and less the much vaguer "Providence." Moreover, after becoming President, Lincoln's speeches take on a more decidedly religious tinge. Lincoln's long-standing belief in his destiny did not change any, but his interpretation as to its source may have.

After the war, Lincoln's personal secretary, John Hay, came across a document in a drawer written in Lincoln's hand. Labeled "Meditations on the Divine Will," this document seems to have never been intended for public consumption. Rather, Lincoln jotted down these words to clarify things in his own mind. It is believed to have been composed in late September 1862, shortly after the Emancipation Proclamation was announced.[85]

Lincoln writes: "The will of God prevails....in the present civil war it is quite possible that God's purpose is something different from the purpose of either party; and yet the human instrumentalities ...are of the best adaptation to effect his purpose." Both sides think God is on their side, Lincoln muses, but in effect he is on neither side.

"God wills this contest," Lincoln continues, "and wills that it shall not end yet. By his mere great power on the minds of the now contestants, he could have either saved or destroyed the Union without a human contest. Yet the contest began. And having begun, he could give the final victory to either side any day. Yet the contest proceeds."[86]

After a year and a half of war, Lincoln's fatalism is clear, but in the "Meditation" there is no longer any hint of "necessity" driven by "motive" and self-interest. Lincoln now seems to regard God as less the disinterested "clock-maker" and more of a very much involved puppet-master, manipulating men and events for a purpose hidden from mortal view. Lincoln's "Meditation" of 1862 focuses on God saving or destroying the Union without mankind actually knowing God's purpose; by March 1865, however, Lincoln seems to have found out that divine purpose:

"If we shall suppose that American Slavery is one of those offences which, in the providence of God, must needs come...He now wills to remove, and that He gives to both North and South, this terrible war as the woe due to those whom the offence came."[87]

In essence, Lincoln tells the nation, slavery was an offence for which both North and South are equally to blame. Now the time has come for God to not only end the offence, but to visit on the Nation a war as the "woe" due it. While Lincoln ends his famous speech talking about charity for all, the bloodletting of the Civil War is clearly viewed by Lincoln as a terrible judgment from God.

To one visitor to the White House at the end of the war, Lincoln compared himself to Moses: "Now I see the end of this terrible conflict with the same joy of Moses at the end of his trying forty years in the wilderness."[88] It is interesting that Lincoln should use that analogy since Moses, too, never lived to see the Promised Land at the end of the journey.

Part and parcel of Lincoln's lifetime faith in his destiny was not only a rise to greatness, but also that he would die once his mission had been fulfilled. Although Lincoln at times made light of this fatal vision, such disavowals seem more have been to allay the fears of others rather than deny it to himself.

Even before taking office as President and then continuing on throughout his presidency, Lincoln's life was threatened on many occasions. His friends and supporters repeatedly urged him to take greater precautions. To one visitor from Kentucky who asked about this, Lincoln replied, "I believe when my time comes there is nothing that I can do to prevent my going."[89]

On another occasion, Lincoln commented half in jest that "if they kill me the next man will be just as bad for them...assassination is always possible, and will come if they are determined upon it."[90]

Many of those around Lincoln also believed in his destiny, foremost among them his wife. Early in the war, Senator Dawes was immediately impressed on meeting him, despite his "unkempt and neglected look." Similarly, Horatio Taft, a War Democrat working for the administration, was also impressed; both Dawes and Taft "were of the opinion that Lincoln was the man sent by Divine Providence to save the country in the dark hours before us."[91] Hence, Lincoln was not alone in believing that his presidency had been foreordained.

If Abraham Lincoln was at times weighed down with the burden of knowing his fate, in a sense it gave him a certain strength that any other man might have lacked. His fatalism gave him the tenacity to weather repeated reverses and disappointments in the knowledge that they were but temporary stumbling blocks on the way to ultimate victory.

While one may cite many logical reasons for Lincoln's sense of destiny, as well as his success in politics and war, for Lincoln himself there was but one underlying cause: he was destined by fate to rise to be president. He was foreordained to lead the nation through its great crisis and, once having brought it safely again to the farther shore, it was also his destiny to die once his mission was accomplished.

That Father Abraham knew all this with a certainty well in advance of events is the great mystery underlying the paranormal Presidency of Abraham Lincoln.

Chapter 12

Liberty and Peace: The Capitol Omen

"Upon whom thou shalt see the Spirit descending as a dove,
and abiding on Him, this is He which baptiseth with the Holy Ghost."

— John 1.33

With the outbreak of the shooting war in the summer of 1861, there were renewed calls in Washington that the reconstruction of the Capitol be halted until the war was over. However, as President Lincoln had said during his inauguration, he viewed the work on the Capitol as a sign — in essence, it was symbolic of his efforts to preserve the Union — and so long as work continued on the building, so, too, would his efforts at rebuilding the nation.

It was no easy task that Lincoln had set, however. In addition to Congress having to transact business there, during the first two years of the war the Capitol was put to military purposes as well.

The Capitol served initially as a fort, with the iron plates of the dome turned into breastworks and artillery peeping through embrasures at every conceivable entrance. After the initial threat to the city had passed, the Capitol was alternately used as barracks, bakery, and hospital by the army. When Congress was in session, the congressmen had to wend their way past large marble blocks, scaffolding, and the din of workmen going to and fro, building the new wings and assembling the massive iron dome.

Atop the new Capitol dome it was planned to mount a statue of liberty — officially called "Freedom Triumphant in War and Peace." The statue had been commissioned before the war; the politician originally charged with overseeing the creation of this statue was a gentleman of the South named Jefferson Davis.

The bronze statue, designed by sculptor Thomas U. Walter, was designed with a "liberty cap" on its head. Jefferson Davis exploded when he saw the design because he knew the "liberty cap" was the old Roman symbol of an emancipated slave! Secretary of War Davis would not tolerate such a symbol; he ordered the northern sculptor to replace the cap with a frilly military helmet.

Casting of the bronze statue was begun in a foundry just outside of Washington in 1860. Ironically, the casting of the statue of liberty was largely carried out by slaves. Progress on casting the massive bronze was initially halted by the outbreak of war, but, by the end of 1862, however, all the parts of the giant liberty were completed.

On December 2nd, to a 35-gun salute, the large bronze casting was hauled atop the completed dome. On hand was a large crowd to witness the ceremony — a ceremony fraught with symbolism. Present in the crowd was Horatio Taft and his teenage daughter.

It took some time for the work crew to install the statue and adjust the last piece of Liberty properly. Finally, as the African American laborers undid the last fastenings of the statue, a white dove appeared out of nowhere.

The white dove circled around the armed Liberty and then at last came to rest on its befeathered head. There were "oohs" and "aahs" in the crowd at the sight of the dove alight on Liberty. "A sign of peace" was on many a tongue at that moment. Mr. Taft turned to his daughter and, knowing her close association with the Lincoln family, said, "You must tell the President."

The appearance of the dove at that precise moment was widely hailed as a sign of coming peace. Although the President was not present himself to witness the incident, he was soon informed. Lincoln already viewed the Capitol as symbolic of the nation as a whole and its rebuilding as a sign of the nation's reconstruction, so the Tafts, father and daughter, knew Lincoln would be interested.

This last, and best, sign upon the Capitol could not have but affirmed Lincoln's belief that both liberty and peace would inevitably be restored once his mission was completed.

Chapter 13

Lincoln and Dreams

"*Sleep hath its own world, And a wide realm of wild reality.*"
— *Byron, "Dreams"*

In our over-medicated modern world, with its fast pace that leaves little time for reflection, sleep is often regarded as that wasted inconvenient interlude between one's waking hours; dreams are merely its irrational by-product.

However, an alternate view holds that dreams are portals to a higher consciousness, not just accidental expressions of the flesh at rest. At times, dreams may convey messages — power even. According to Dr. Larry Dossey, a respected scientist who has studied the issue, dreams of future events constitute more than half the ESP experiences that people report.[92]

Abraham Lincoln was a great believer in the meaning of dreams. According to one contemporary, who observed both the President and Mrs. Lincoln closely: "Mrs. Lincoln believed in signs, but the President believed in dreams."[93] As the President once explained, "In the old days God and His angels came to men in their sleep and made themselves known through dreams." Then, half apologetically, Lincoln added, "Nowadays dreams are regarded as very foolish and are seldom told, except by old women and by young men and maidens in love."[94]

Lincoln would commonly begin a recitation of a disturbing dream to his wife and then discount its importance. Yet clearly Lincoln put a great deal of stock in his dreams, many of which were clearly of an ominous character.

While Freudian analysts have had a field day applying their theories to Lincoln — especially to his relationships with women — other schools of psychology in recent years have begun to weigh in on the sixteenth president, especially regarding his faith in dreams. Karl Jung was one of the pioneers in exploring the spiritual side of the human psyche, as opposed to Freud's obsession with the sexual side; since him various other psychological schools have explored the spiritual aspects of human experience and their expression in dreams.

These branches of modern psychology view dreams as something more than the babbling of the irrational subconscious. Indeed, some hold that certain dreams arise from a source beyond reason, from a greater reality not accessible by the conscious mind, but are nonetheless quite coherent and lucid. There are many categories of lucid dreaming, but for our purposes there are four that seem to relate to those in which Lincoln experienced: dreams of visitation, dreams of parental concern, predictive dreams, and dreams of prophecy.

Commonly, a dream of visitation involves a deceased loved one — a close relative, friend, or lover who has recently died. Such dreams, very vivid in appearance, often have a consoling effect on the person experiencing them. The apparition appears absolutely real, as if the person is still living and present with them.

While the Lincolns lost their young son Eddie to disease in 1850, it was the death of William Wallace Lincoln in February of 1861 that seemed to have had a devastating effect on both Abraham and Mary.

Mrs. Lincoln had always been high-strung and emotional; some historians think the death of Willie pushed her over the edge and that she had a nervous breakdown as a result. However, Lincoln felt the loss of Willie just as deeply as his wife; with the strain of conducting the war, it's a wonder that he didn't break down as well. However, due to his nature, Lincoln handled the loss differently. He became more introspective, more contemplative — and he began to dream about Willie.

Colonel LeGrand B. Cannon, a military aide to Lincoln, would occasionally be privy to Lincoln's personal comments and observations. One time, Lincoln was reading from Shakespeare — his favorite source of literary entertainment next to the Bible — and he came across a passage from a play where the mother mourns the death of her son.

The passage started Lincoln thinking about Willie. He then confided to Colonel Cannon: "Did you ever dream of some lost friend and feel you were having a sweet communion with him?....That is the way I dream of my lost boy Willie."[95] After Lincoln uttered those words, he was overcome with emotion; he bowed down his head and sobbed out loud.

How many times Willie came to Lincoln in his dreams is not known, but apparently it was frequent in the year after he died. For Lincoln, these visitations were a bittersweet reunion.

Mary was also visited by Willie after his death. In Mrs. Lincoln's case, though, it is not entirely certain whether Willie came to her in her dreams or as a waking vision.

When her sister Emilie visited the White House in the fall of 1863, Mary confessed to her that Willie visited her on a regular basis. "Willie lives," Mary told Emilie. "He comes to me every night and stands at the foot of the bed with his same sweet, adorable smile he has always had."[96]

In the case of Mary, Willie was accompanied on occasion by "little Eddie" and at least twice by her brother, Alexander Todd, who had been a lieutenant in the Confederate army and was killed in combat in August 1862. Mary told her sister, "You cannot dream of the comfort this gives me. When I thought of my little son in immensity, alone...it nearly broke my heart."[97]

Clearly, both Mary and Abraham experienced visitations from Willie of some nature. Their grieving for Willie was not assuaged completely by their "sweet communion" in dreams alone, however, as they both turned elsewhere for continuing contact with their son. Lincoln is also on record as having experienced several dreams of caution during his time at the White House.

In June 1863, Mary had left Washington with their son Tad and went to Philadelphia for a visit. Like many modern wives, when Mary Lincoln was feeling depressed, she would go on a shopping spree, either to Philadelphia or New York, and shop her way out of the blues. Like many a modern husband, Lincoln would often become vexed at his wife's excessive spending.

While Mary and Tad were away on this particular occasion, Lincoln had a disturbing dream. The dream cautioned him about Tad's possession of a pistol. In 1861, Julia Taft tells us,

Tad "had a terrible longing for what he called a 'real revolver' (one that would shoot)." Tad kept pestering his parents until they finally gave him a working pistol.

On the frontier, it was not unusual for young boys to handle guns, but they were expected to know how to handle them safely. Apparently Tad was not up to the task, despite giving his father his "after-David."[98]

We are not privy to the details of Lincoln's dream, but it was apparently sufficiently disturbing that Lincoln sent his wife an urgent telegram on June 9th: "Think you better put Tad's pistol away. I had an ugly dream about him."[99]

In another case, Lincoln was visiting City Point, Virginia. During the final phase of the war, City Point was the Union army's major base of operations for the siege of Richmond. While there, Lincoln again had a vivid dream.

In his dream, the President saw the White House consumed in flames. Lincoln was so upset by his nightmare that he dispatched his wife "up the river" back to Washington. Following her husband's explicit instructions, she met Secretary of War Stanton and was escorted to the White House to see in person that it was intact and undamaged. Only then did Mary wire her husband that everything was alright.[100]

Lincoln's predictive dream about the White House proved not to be true, but one psychologist who has investigated such phenomena avers that such predictive dreams "anticipate the trajectory of current events and picture the likely outcome." This sort of dream projects a "probable future" in order to *prevent* it from coming to fruition.[101]

Another interpretation has been proposed for this dream as well. It has been suggested that Parson Weems' *Life of George Washington* may have been the unconscious inspiration for Lincoln's dream. While Weems' biography is no longer taken as serious history, his book did collect a number of legends and folktales current in the early nineteenth century about the first president. Among these tales was one about a dream of Washington's house burning; at the time it was interpreted as a prophetic dream about the coming of the Civil War.[102]

It is certainly possible that Lincoln's subconscious summoned up a passage in Weems' book that he had read in his youth and spun it into a realistic dream. With all of his concerns about prosecuting the war, dreaming about the "house divided" in flames would not have been so far-fetched a notion.

One could take Lincoln's dream of the White House burning more literally, however. Throughout the war, Washington, D.C. remained a hotbed of Secessionism. Although many left the city to join the Confederate Army in the spring of 1861, there still remained a large fifth column within the city watching and waiting, hoping to harm the Federal government and its elected officials. We only know of John Wilkes Booth's Rebel cell because they succeeded. There were other agents at work; that one or another might set fire to the White House hoping to catch Lincoln napping was something well within the realm of possibility.

While modern psychology may explain away some of Lincoln's uncanny dreams, other such dreams resist easy interpretations. As we shall see, towards the end of Lincoln's presidency, he experienced several prophetic dreams that weighed heavily upon him — and upon us too.

To understand Lincoln's belief regarding his uncanny dreams, one should take note of the poem alluded to at the outset. If we trust those closest to the great man, Byron's "Dreams" was a favorite of Lincoln's. It perhaps most closely expresses his attitude on the subject:

> *"And dreams in their*
> *development have breath,*
> *And tears and tortures, and the*
> *touch of joy;*
> *They leave a weight upon our*
> *waking thoughts,*
> *They take a weight from off our*
> *waking toils,*
> *The do divide our being."*

Chapter 14

Lincoln and the Rise of Spiritualism

"Death, the Undiscovered Country from whose bourn no traveler returns."

— William Shakespeare, Hamlet

Perhaps no aspect of the paranormal presidency of Abraham Lincoln is quite so controversial as his relationship with Spiritualism. Even during Lincoln's lifetime it was at times a contentious issue. After his passing, there were those who took umbrage at the mere possibility that the sixteenth president attended séances and communed with mediums, much less that he may even himself have been a devotee of the movement.

Most modern biographers and virtually all academic purveyors of Lincolnalia have firmly rejected any notion that Lincoln was connected to the Spiritualist movement out of hand. Beginning with Nicholas and Hay's ten-volume official biography and continuing on through to today's weighty tomes, a standard portrait of Lincoln has been cast that leaves little room for such heterodox practices as Spiritualism in the great man's life. A typical example of this is Lincoln scholar Jay Monaghan's classic essay on the subject — in the first sentence he characterizes all proponents of Lincoln as a Spiritualist as "detractors."[103]

While those who have made the case for Lincoln as a Spiritualist often have made some strident claims, right or wrong, very few of them were attempting to denigrate or demean Abraham Lincoln. Quite the contrary, the proponents of Lincoln as an active participant in séances and believer in spirit communications seem mainly motivated by a desire to embrace the sixteenth president as one of their own. By their lights, Lincoln being a Spiritualist is a positive attribute.

Given the biases that still exist regarding Lincoln's relationship with séances, mediums, and Spiritualism, it is important to look at the movement within the social, political, and intellectual context of the era and with as little modern ideological baggage as possible. Where did this seemingly unorthodox movement come from and how did American culture view it in the middle decades of the nineteenth century?

It may come as a surprise to some modern readers that the séance is a uniquely American invention. Of course, humans have been seeking to make contact with the spirits of the dead for millennia; entering into trance-like states or other altered states of consciousness probably goes back as far as the Mesolithic era. In the Old Testament, King Saul consults the Witch of Endor to summon the shade of the Prophet Isaiah with unhappy results. St. Augustine, writing in the fifth century AD, tells us of similar efforts by his contemporaries: "The spirits of the dead can be sent to the living and can unveil to them the future which they themselves have learned from other spirits or from angels or by divine revelation."[104] However, the origin of the séance and the Spiritualist movement can be traced to the late 1840s, to a small town in upstate New York.

Hydesville was a small hamlet some twenty miles outside Rochester, New York. On December 11, 1847, John Fox and his family moved into their new home in that village. On their very first night in the house, however, inexplicable sounds were heard throughout; there were knocking sounds and the windows rattled violently.

John Fox was a no-nonsense sort of fellow, a blacksmith by trade; he attributed the night-time noises to loose floorboards. He spent the next day securing everything in the house that might possibly vibrate or rattle. However, the next night, the Fox family was again subjected to the strange shake, rattle, and roll of the house. Mr. Fox soon found out that the previous resident of the house, Michael Weekman, had moved out shortly before because of the uncanny sounds of rapping, invisible footsteps padding about the house, and unearthly dragging sounds. It turned out that reports of poltergeist activity in the house dated back to at least 1843.

Although the sounds were heard throughout the house, the poltergeist activity seemed to focus on the two youngest daughters of the family, Kate, age 12, and Maggie, age 15. The Foxs' haunting shared at least one attribute common to many poltergeist infestations: the presence of adolescents or children about to go through puberty.

Although the Foxes were well-respected members of the Methodist Church, Mrs. Fox came from a family whose female members from the three previous generations all had a reputation for being able to predict deaths, births, and other happenings. Moreover, that part of New York was a region referred to as the "burnt over district" because religious fads and cults had a habit of arising there and spreading like wildfire.

As winter edged into spring, the Fox family gradually got used to the nightly disturbances and came to accept the fact that they were not caused by loose board, local pranksters, or anything of this world. The two Fox sisters even gave the poltergeist a name — "Mr. Splitfoot."

Gradually, the sisters came to realize that they could communicate with the mysterious spirit and developed a code: one rap for yes, two raps for no. Ultimately their older brother David worked out a system using the letters of the alphabet to spell out words — a primitive version of the *ouija*.

Thinking the poltergeist activity in the house would cease if they sent Kate and Maggie away to stay with their older sister Leah, the parents packed them off to Rochester. However, the rapping and other uncanny activities continued in the house; not only that, but the poltergeist apparently also followed the sisters to the big city as well.

Leah Fox Underhill was a 33-year-old divorced single mother who eked out a living teaching music. She was also a devotee of the self-anointed mystic and prophet, Andrew Jackson Davis, who wrote extensively about such wild-eyed ideas as evolution, the use of electricity for transportation, communications, and music, and his own version of a Unified Field Theory. Davis's ideas about life after death were influenced by the writings of eighteenth century Swedish metaphysical philosopher Emmanuel Swedenborg, who had a near-death experience earlier in his life and wrote about "crossing over" and argued for the nearness of the spirit realm to the material world.

Leah saw in her sisters' ability to contact "Mr. Splitfoot" (and apparently other spirits) as the fulfillment of one of Andrew Jackson Davis's prophecies. She saw in their occult talents a way to promote her spiritual ideas, not to mention to make some much-needed money. After meeting with initial skepticism, the Fox sisters' innovative techniques of spirit communication finally found acceptance and a wider audience. Some of the early converts to the Fox sisters' system of spirit communications were a local faction of Quakers dissatisfied with their sect's passivity in regards to moral issues of the day such as slavery. They were referred to in some quarters as "Quakers with muscles."

Within only a few short years, the Fox sisters' séances began attracting intellectual, political, and business leaders. The likes of James Fenimore Cooper, Horace Greeley, William Lloyd Garrison, Sojourner Truth, and William Cullen Bryant all went to see the Foxes. In particular, wealthy patrons who had lost loved ones consulted the two young girls and subsidized their activities.

In no time, the Fox sisters' success inspired others of similar ilk; soon there were all manner of mediums plying their craft all across the Republic. Indeed, with a kind of missionary fervor, mediums and "trance lecturers" traveled to Europe to spread their message. The innovation from upstate New York was rapidly becoming an international phenomenon.

Mrs. Lincoln is generally given credit — or blame — for being the first First Lady to frequent a medium. Not true: Jane Appleton Pierce earns the prize of first place in this regard.

The wife of the fourteenth president had already lost two of her three children before they reached the age of five. Her surviving son, Benjamin Pierce, was traveling on a train with her just weeks before her husband's inauguration when, tragically, their train derailed and young Ben was crushed to death in the wreck. Although her husband now occupied the White House, Mrs. Pierce remained reclusive, inconsolable, and mourning for her son. However, in 1853, the one solace Mrs. Pierce finally found in her grief was by consulting famed medium Maggie Fox.

Mrs. Pierce was not unique: almost from the first, those who lost a close family member or loved one had recourse to the services of a medium. The many contagious diseases and plagues that raged unchecked, such as typhus, yellow fever, smallpox, or diphtheria, meant that the death of a child or spouse was a commonplace, albeit tragic, event in ante-bellum America.

At the same time, however, séances were also embraced as a form of popular entertainment. To promote their innovative means of contacting the spirits, the Foxes began performing at Corinthian Hall in Rochester in 1849. When he heard about the Fox sisters' remarkable stage performances, none other than P. T. Barnum recruited them and put them on the boards in New York City. This set the stage (literally) for other mediums to emulate them throughout the country — and soon throughout the world.

In addition to the spread of professional mediums such as the Fox sisters, others soon found they could communicate with the dead and exhibit other paranormal phenomena. Nothing succeeds like excess, and soon a whole host of amateur mediums arose almost overnight. In Ohio, during the 1850s, says novelist William Dean Howells in *The Undiscovered Country*, in his youth it seemed to him as though virtually every household had its own medium and "tipping table."[105] While many took séances and Spiritualism quite seriously, other Americans came to regard it as a form of parlor entertainment.

By the eve of the Rebellion, the influence of Spiritualism had spread far and wide. It is estimated that before the Civil War as much as ten percent of the American public were involved in Spiritualism in one way or another. Princess Salm-Salm, who, contrary to her married title, was of Canadian extraction and married to a Union officer, observed that "the spiritualist epidemic was then commencing to rage in America, one heard nothing but of spirits and mediums. All tables and other furniture seemed to have become alive and you could not sit down upon a chair without a spiritual suspicion."[106]

The outbreak of the war, with its terrible loss of life, further stimulated interest in Spiritualism. In one New York newspaper, on a given day in 1862, one could see ads for as many as four medical clairvoyants, twelve public mediums, and four "spiritualistic associations" within its pages.[107]

On the face of it, therefore, there would have been nothing unusual for the Lincolns to have at least attended séances, if not actually become confirmed believers. Indeed, many mainstream Protestant clergy embraced Spiritualism as positive proof of the afterlife and as a way to combat religious skepticism and the epidemic of "freethinkers" who doubted the tenets of Christianity.

It is mainly in the postwar era, when some Spiritualists seeking greater legitimacy, formed their own "churches" that we find many mainstream preachers begin to see it as a threat and the idea that Lincoln may have attended séances came to be regarded as a scandal to be suppressed. This inconvenient truth also got in the way of many Protestant clergy trying to convert Lincoln post-mortem to their faith. Similarly, stage magicians, seeing the Spiritualists' stage performances as a threat to their business, likewise took a hostile stance to it — an attitude that persists today.

When it comes to documenting the Lincolns' involvement with mediums and séances, one is, therefore, confronted with widely differing statements by contemporaries. Robert Todd Lincoln, the Lincolns' only son to survive to adulthood, was very much the gatekeeper of the Lincoln legacy and zealous in his efforts to maintain the image of his father's post-mortem orthodoxy. When a leading psychic who knew Lincoln came out with her memoirs, Robert roundly denounced her claims in no uncertain terms: "Ex-Minister Robert T. Lincoln is at pains to deny (that Lincoln was a Spiritualist). He says there is not an iota of truth in the story."[108]

John G. Nicolay, Lincoln's private secretary and co-author of a highly censored (by Robert Lincoln) ten-volume biography of the sixteenth president that stands as the quasi-official biography of Abraham Lincoln, also denied the President's involvement with Spiritualism: "I never knew of his attending a séance of Spiritualists at the White House or elsewhere," he said on one occasion. However, Nicolay's denial was a nuanced one, for he goes on to say, "Of course, I have no doubt that Mr. Lincoln, like a great many other men, *might* have had some curiosity as to spiritualism, and *might* have attended some of the séances solely out of curiosity...*if* President Lincoln ever attended séances...it was with this same feeling of curiosity."[109]

At the opposite extreme, many spiritualists over the last century and a half have claimed Lincoln as one of their own, some stridently so. Some of this is based on "spectral evidence," as some spiritualists have communed with the dead president themselves. Unfortunately, spectral evidence is also what got the Puritan judges in seventeenth century Salem in trouble — or rather their innocent victims.

However, there were others present when Lincoln attended séances: "There can be no question but that Mr. Lincoln sat in séances and repeatedly had mediums at the White House."[110] One eyewitness even claimed that a medium single-handedly inspired Lincoln to issue the Emancipation Proclamation.[111] Other spiritualists made further claims regarding both the Lincolns' involvement with séances and Spiritualism.

Given such widely divergent claims about Lincoln and the "Spirit Rappers," what is one to believe about this aspect of the paranormal presidency? Is this just wishful thinking on the part of adherents of Spiritualism or is there solid evidence regarding Lincoln's relationship with the Spiritualists?

Those few mainstream historians willing to concede limited participation on the part of Lincoln in séances generally limit it to the period following the death of his son Willie in February 1862 — and that his motive was only to humor his grief-crazed wife — with emphasis on the crazy part. However, there is contemporary evidence that does indicate that Lincoln was in close contact with mediums well before Willie's death.

We have, for example, the testimony of a certain Colonel Simon P. Kase, who was not only an expert in railroad operations, but also a confirmed believer in Spiritualism. Early in the war he was in Washington D.C. on business, with an appointment to meet with the President. He was walking down Pennsylvania Avenue one day, headed towards the Capitol, when he noticed a nameplate on the front of a building where he used to room. The nameplate read, he tells us, "H. Conkling" (actually the name was H. B. Conklin) and, whether moved by curiosity or an unseen spirit guide, Kase was drawn inside to see who lived there now. There, he made the acquaintance of the "writing medium" Conklin and, although they had never met before, Conklin prevailed on the Colonel to deliver a letter of introduction from him to the President.

Curiously, though the medium had accompanied Colonel Kase to the White House, he stayed in an adjoining parlor while Kase had a personal audience with Lincoln and delivered Conklin's letter. Although Conklin was actually present, according to Kase, Lincoln set up an appointment to meet with the medium for the following Sunday. More curiously, Kase insisted that the President draft a written reply to Conklin.[112]

Colonel Kase wrote his accounts of Lincoln's encounters with mediums much later in life and apparently by that point his memory was somewhat muddled, especially with regard to dates. As a result, Kase's testimony seems in error on some points, although he was an honest reporter of what he remembered. It would be easy enough for a skeptic to dismiss Kase's Conklin account as fantasy if we did not have documented evidence contemporary with the event to corroborate it.

In the Library of Congress, among their vast collection of papers relating to Abraham Lincoln, is, in fact, preserved the very letter by Conklin that Kase handed to the President. Dated December 28, 1861, with a return address in New York (where Conklin actually resided at the time), Conklin's missive is actually a cover letter for another message, sent by Lincoln's close friend Edward Baker — Baker was unable to deliver his message in person because he had

died two months before at the Battle of Ball's Bluff.[113]

The document substantiates Colonel Kase's narrative, although it points up some of his errors: the letter is dated late in 1861 whereas the good Colonel remembered the incident as occurring sometime in 1862…just four weeks before Lincoln's first encounter with the medium Nettie Colburn. (Kase also erred about the date of Miss Colburn's first encounter with the President.) Nevertheless, the incident was real and proves a definitive contact between the medium and Lincoln.

In addition to this incident, we also have a report of an even earlier date that indicates prior contact between the President and Conklin. A newspaper article entitled, "The President Elect a Spiritualist," was published early in March 1861, in which Conklin claimed to have met Lincoln in New York the previous March and provided Mr. Lincoln with information from another deceased friend. In this case, the article describes Lincoln as still "President Elect," so even if Conklin's chronology is off, the incident still would have taken place well before his inauguration.[114]

The upshot of the whole Conklin story not only illustrates the hazards of relying solely on postwar memories of events, but it also highlights the folly of dismissing such recollections out of hand. The letters from Conklin were real; they were delivered to Lincoln, and Conklin was in contact with Lincoln. It may well be, too, that Conklin first had contact with Lincoln prior to his election. Other evidence indicates Lincoln attended at least one Conklin séance in Washington as well.[115]

Also dating to before Lincoln's inauguration is a communication, from December 1860, by a person in Cleveland with the initials "G.A." Identifying himself as "Wide Awake," G. A. relayed a warning of a conspiracy to assassinate "Your Excellancy" (Lincoln). The informant for G.A.'s alleged plot was a young girl who resided in his household whom he describes as a "Somnambulist" and a "Clairvoyant"; however, he rejects the appellation "Spiritualist." While in a trance, the young girl relayed news of a plot to poison Lincoln. Interestingly, the author of the warning letter was a loyal Republican and a firm believer in paranormal phenomena, but hostile to the Spiritualist movement.[116]

Though we can't be certain how extensive Lincoln's early relationship with Spiritualism was, there is additional evidence that his interest in Spiritualism extended well beyond the passive receipt of letters — and dated to well before his election.

In a long-forgotten interview with Lincoln's old law partner Herndon, a reporter not only transcribed Herndon's opinions about his old friend, but also transcribed an exact list of the books sitting on the bookshelf of their old law office, most of which had been there gathering dust ever since Lincoln had left to become President. While the Lincoln-Herndon law office contained much of what one would expect in such an establishment, there were many tomes clearly to the tastes of Abraham Lincoln's broad interests

that had nothing to do with law, politics, or oratory.

One finds, for example, books of poetry, science, moralistic essays, and books on Temperance, but also Thomas Paine's works. Two volumes listed on Lincoln's bookshelf leap off the pages of the newspaper interview, however. On the very top shelf of Lincoln's bookcase sits Robert D. Owens' *Footfalls on the Boundary of Another World* (1859) and just below on the second shelf is Volume III of Andrew Jackson Davis' multi-volume work, "The Great Harmonia," the tome titled *The Seer* (1852).[117]

Robert Dale Owen was a political activist with a strong interest in both Abolitionism and Spiritualism and someone well known to Lincoln. The presence of his book on Spiritualism on Lincoln's shelf, however, is surprising. Davis, as we've seen, was a seer and prophet who influenced the early Spiritualists; he was in fact a seminal thinker whose metaphysical ideas ante-dated the whole Spiritualist movement.

In 1874, Mary Lincoln indicated to John Todd Stuart that Herndon had "stolen" her husband's law books and their private library; Mrs. Lincoln and Herndon never were on good terms, but her statement corroborates that the bulk of the books in the office were indeed her husband's. In legal terms, although the presence of Spiritualism books on Lincoln's bookshelves are not in themselves sufficient circumstantial evidence to convict Lincoln of being a Spiritualist, they are certainly sufficient to indict.

There is yet another pre-inaugural incident tying the Great Emancipator to Spiritualism. When Lincoln was traveling to Washington to be inaugurated in early 1861, a plot was uncovered to assassinate him while he was passing through Baltimore. Precautions had to be taken to divert attention from his passage and he was coerced into adopting a disguise that made him look like an 1861 version of Sherlock Holmes. His traveling in mufti was the source of much ridicule by his political enemies at the time, but the threat was apparently real enough. It was later claimed, however, that the medium Charles Redmond's premonition was what actually forewarned Lincoln of the assassination plot.

Better documented, however, is a warning from the Spiritualist community dated later that year. In a letter dated August 9, 1861, a certain J.B. Hastings of Boston, Massachusetts, who described himself as "an undoubting believer in Spirit Communication," transmitted a warning to Lincoln by way of the Secretary of the Interior, Caleb B. Smith.

The person who was actually gifted with "second sight," according to the letter, was one G.M. Laren, whom Hastings affirmed was of "high character." Laren had apparently predicted the Union's defeat at Bull Run several days before the battle using second sight, with "visions... of sheep fleeing in all directions to represent the federal army."

Hastings was writing to Lincoln to warn him of an "eminent danger" to his life and that of General Scott.

Laren had told him: "The President was surrounded with traitors in disguise" who intended to blow up buildings in the capitol, to be followed up by a Confederate attack on Washington.[118]

The visionary Laren seems to have been sincere enough, as was the unnamed girl gifted with clairvoyance. Strictly speaking, however, although believing to possess psychic gifts, neither could really be called mediums since it was not spirits of the dead that informed them of these plots; instead, they came to them by their own inner gifts of second sight.

As to the accuracy of such psychic warnings, we shall never know. There were indeed a number of plots to kill Lincoln, not only early in the war but also throughout the conflict. All during the war, Washington was a hotbed of secessionist sympathizers and there may well have been any number of such plots that never got beyond the planning stage.

What is interesting about the Hastings letter is that it was transmitted to the President through his Secretary of Interior, Caleb Smith. Secretary Smith was a Mid-Western Republican who had been instrumental in Lincoln obtaining the Republican nomination in 1860. How Hastings knew Smith is unknown, but it is reasonable to assume that Smith was known to the Spiritualist community as a friend, if not one of their own. Nor would Smith be the only Lincoln Cabinet member with links to Spiritualism.

Mr. Hastings' letter gives us some insight into his background; for one thing he tells us his late son had been a Presbyterian minister. The fact that many church-going folk of this era could also be Spiritualists is not all that unusual. In Washington, too, there were members of the Presbyterian Church who were also dedicated Spiritualists.

Although a number of names are mentioned in connection with the President and Mrs. Lincoln's frequenting of mediums during the war, the names that seem to arise most often are the Lauries. Reference to Cranston and Margaret Laurie occur in various sources relating to the subject. Their household in Georgetown was apparently a hub of Spiritualist activity in Washington during the war.

In evaluating the legitimacy of claims of the President attending séances at the Laurie household, we need to look more closely at the Laurie clan. What sort of folk were the Lauries? Were they crass opportunists out to make fame and fortune by gulling the credulous? Or were they genuine explorers of the Undiscovered Country, seeking to make contact with the other side and help loved ones get in touch with family or friends who had passed over?

Looking at the documentary record, we find that Cranston Laurie was a senior clerk in the Washington D.C. offices of the U. S. Postal Service. In those days, the title "clerk" could often refer to a bureaucrat of high station and, since he held a post in the office of the statistician, one gathers that he did more than just dispense stamps. He joined the Post Office in 1834 and remained a dedicated civil servant for a number of years after the war, dying in 1880. Moreover, Cranston Laurie

was the son of the Reverend Dr. James Laurie, a highly esteemed Presbyterian minister and the founding pastor of the F Street Presbyterian Church, which later became the New York Avenue Presbyterian Church. This is the same church that came to be known as "The Church of Presidents."[119]

Cranston had married Miss Margaret Ann McCutcheon in 1832 and the couple had two sons: Lewis, born in 1846, and James (or Jack) born in 1848. The Lauries also had a daughter named Emma. Born Emma Francis Smitson in 1852, her parents apparently died when she was quite young and she seems to have been adopted by a gentleman named William Mockabee, who listed her in his will in 1859. In the 1860 census, she was listed as Emma Francis Mockabee. By 1862, however, Emma was in the Cranston household. They apparently also adopted Emma, as when she married Thomas H. Rudderforth in 1873, her maiden name was listed as Emma Francis Laurie.[120]

All in all, the picture one gains of the Laurie family is of a respected and well established Washington family whose careers were dedicated to serving the public. They were clergymen, civil servants, and loyal citizens; they were hardly the "charlatans" or "flum-masters" that some historians have cavalierly labeled them.

Margaret Laurie discovered her gifts as a medium sometime in the 1850s. While Cranston never professed to have any psychic powers himself, he was an active supporter of the movement and his wife's paranormal gifts.

How Emma came to be adopted remains obscure; it may have been that Emma's psychic abilities had come to their attention and her parent-less state made them seem pre-ordained to become her parents. In any case, Emma was still only ten years old in 1862, when the Lauries' séances with the Lincolns comes to the public's attention.

Mentioned as a "daughter" by some eyewitnesses is an adult female who went by the name of Mrs. Belle Miller; she was what was called a "physical medium" and was apparently quite good at her craft. She is reported to have been married to a retired steamboat captain. Her actual relationship to the Laurie family remains obscure.

The Cranstons' son Jack, in a notarized statement dating to 1885, verifies the fact that the President and Mrs. Lincoln attended séances in their household. He states that "from early in 1862 to late in 1863" Lincoln visited their household to attend séances and that "during portions of the time such visits were very frequent." Jack goes on to say: "My father became personally acquainted with the late President Abraham Lincoln and my belief is that through my father's influence, the President became interested in Spiritualism."[121]

One may well wonder how a postal clerk — even a senior clerk — made the acquaintance of the President and the First Lady. While this aspect remains mysterious, the answer may well lay in the fact that Cranston was the son of the Reverend James Laurie, the founder of the New York Avenue Presbyterian Church. Dr. Laurie served as pastor of the church from 1803 until his death in 1853. Presumably, Cranston and his wife continued to be good, church-going folk after his father's death. We know for a fact that the Lincolns started renting a pew in the New York Avenue Presbyterian Church beginning in June 1861. One researcher has characterized this church as "a Mecca for New Agers of the era." Clearly, Mr. and Mrs. Laurie were the main movers behind the "New Age" circle within the congregation.

Interestingly enough, the minister who succeeded Reverend Laurie after his death was a divine, the Reverend Dr. Phineas D. Gurley, and it was the Reverend Gurley who headed the New York Avenue congregation throughout the Civil War. It was also Reverend Gurley who laid claim to President Lincoln being a member of his church and a confirmed Christian. It was the good reverend who also emphatically stated that "Mr. Lincoln was greatly annoyed by the report that he was interested in spiritualism."[122] It is quite true that the President rented a pew in Reverend Gurley's church and attended services there; however, there is no truth whatsoever to the claim that Lincoln was ever a confirmed Christian of any sect.

When their son Willie died in February 1862, the Reverend Gurley presided at the funeral service. No doubt both the Lincolns found spiritual solace attending church there, but the Reverend Gurley was apparently not the only one providing solace in his congregation. We may presume that Dr. Phineas was oblivious to the fact that the son of his predecessor

The "Lincoln Pew," in the original New York Avenue Presbyterian Church in Washington D.C., was used by the Lincolns during the war. Although the President and First Lady attended church here, Lincoln was not a devout Christian as its pastor, the Reverend Phineas Gurley, later asserted. The Rev. Gurley also denied that Lincoln had ever attended any séances when, in fact, Lincoln and several other respected members of this congregation attended séances during the war and were deeply involved in the Spiritualism movement, including the son of its previous pastor, Cranston Laurie.

and others of his flock were active Spiritualists. If Rev. Gurley could talk about life after death to the Lincolns when their son Willie died, the Lauries could demonstrate it to them.

There were important political dimensions to the Spiritualist movement, both in Washington and elsewhere throughout the land. There was, in fact, a strong correlation between many who were active in Spiritualism in the period leading up to the war and other progressive political causes, such as the abolition of slavery and women's rights.

According to Dr. Fayette Hall, a lapsed Spiritualist turned Lincoln-hater, at a séance at the Lauries' *prior* to Lincoln's nomination, one of the Lauries went into a trance and contacted the spirit of Robert Rantoul, who predicted that Lincoln would not only be nominated but elected President as well. Dr. Hall credits this séance as the true cause of Lincoln's meteoric political rise from obscurity.[123]

Whether Lincoln was actively involved with the Spiritualists at such an early date is still a moot point. However, the Spiritualist circles in Washington, Chicago, New York, Boston, and elsewhere in the North were certainly aware of Lincoln and his stance regarding slavery. Besides the Lauries, another active Spiritualist whom Dr. Hall knew well was Judge Augustus Wattles. During the summers of 1863 and 1864, Wattles spent a considerable time with Hall and informed him much of both spiritual and political affairs. Wattles had also spent substantial time visiting the Lauries, where, we are informed, "There was very little of any importance occurring in which he was not informed."

Wattles had been born in Connecticut, but came to maturity in the Midwest and entered Lane Theological Seminary to study for the Presbyterian ministry. It was at this time that Wattles became heavily involved in abolitionism. While Wattles was engaged in missionary work among both whites and blacks in Ohio, Augustus also started becoming active in the Spiritualist movement there. After a tragedy occurred to a local group of his Spiritualist followers, Augustus and his brother John moved to Kansas, where they soon became heavily embroiled in the Free Soil movement. Wattles worked with "General" Jim Lane and John Brown in Kansas battling pro-slavery vigilantes and helping runaway slaves escape to Canada.

Jim Lane, it should be noted, was not only a militant foe of the pro-slavery "Border Ruffians" in Kansas, but during the early days of the Lincoln presidency he also commanded a force of volunteer "militia" — the "Frontier Guard" — in Washington to protect the President's person. In the first few days of the Lincoln presidency, there was a substantial number of rabid secessionist sympathizers throughout the city and few regular army troops available, as no state troops had yet arrived.

For several critical weeks, "General" Lane's little *freikorps* were among the few loyal troops on hand to protect Lincoln and Washington. What exact role Augustus Wattles had in obtaining Lane's force is not known, but we do know that it was Wattles who introduced Colonel Kase to Mrs. Laurie and the Washington Spiritualists in 1861.

Wattles certainly was not the only abolitionist leader to be also a leader in the Spiritualist movement. Lincoln's friend, Robert Dale Owen of Indiana, was a progressive politician with substantial credentials not only opposing slavery, but fighting for women's rights, as well as a fervent proponent of Socialism. His father had founded the New Harmony Commune in Indiana and while that experiment did not last, his son remained a militant activist throughout his life. As we've seen, Robert Dale Owen was deep into Spiritualism and had also counseled medium Margaret Fox.

Horace Greeley, the famed crusading New York newspaper publisher, was a strong advocate of abolitionism and threw his weight behind Lincoln for president; Greeley was also an active enthusiast of Spiritualism. Nor was Greeley alone; in New York, many politicians and decision-makers opposed to slavery were also active in

Spiritualism. In New England the tale was much the same: many leaders of the abolition and Free Soil movements — including many Protestant clergy — were enthusiastic spiritualists.

The Hutchinson Family Singers, from New Hampshire, were nationally known performers. Their song, *For Lincoln and Liberty Too*, motivated many citizens to come out and vote for the *Son of Kentucky* in November 1861, and they were unabashed foes of slavery. However, the Hutchinsons were also Spiritualists and penned another song advocating that movement as well.

All this is not to say that *all* Spiritualists were "for Lincoln and Liberty too." In the years before the war, there was a lively debate in the pages of William Lloyd Garrison's *The Liberator* regarding relations between Spiritualism and Abolitionism. Some Northern Spiritualists were loath to criticize their Southern brethren who were decidedly pro-slavery. One defender of these less progressive Spiritualists — Warren Chase — argued that "I cannot separate myself from my race or nation, because there are slaveholders and rumsellers in it; I cannot separate myself from Spiritualists or Spiritualism, because they are Democrats and Whigs and Know Nothings..."[124]

The basic fact is that the devotees of Spiritualism and similar practices in the 1850s were not woolly-minded social misfits or dropouts; rather, they were political activists, business and political leaders, and prominent intellectuals of the day. They were in essence a substantial part of the Northern social and economic elite and a force to be reckoned with. The overall picture of the movement is that Spiritualists constituted a powerful network of potential king-makers — if a clever politician could tap into it. Perhaps Lincoln did.

Chapter 15

All the President's Mediums

"Softly, softly, hear the rustle
Of the Spirits airy wings;
They are coming down to mingle
Once again with earthly things...
Ra-tap-tap lost friends are near you.
Rap-tap-tap they see and hear you..."

— "Spirit Rappings," 1853
Lyrics by J. E. Garrett

As we have seen, the accepted wisdom regarding Lincoln and Spiritualism is in error. Nevertheless, the thesis that the President's minimal involvement with séances and mediums was due to humoring a grief-crazed wife still holds court in most academic circles. While it is true that Mary Todd Lincoln did have recourse to mediums, the preponderance of evidence shows that her husband was as much involved with mediums as Mary, perhaps even more so.

How early Lincoln was interested in Spiritualism and exactly what his motivations were behind it remains moot. Certainly his long-standing faith in prophetic dreams, omens, visions, and other paranormal phenomena would have recommended the movement to his attention, since the Spiritualists shared most such beliefs. We know that he was familiar with at least some of the ideas of Andrew Jackson Davis, the intellectual godfather of the movement. Moreover, Lincoln's firm political stand against slavery and his belief that it was a moral wrong were values he held in common with most persons involved in the movement in the northern states. Certainly Lincoln had to have been aware that many of his friends and political allies were also Spiritualists.

It is, of course, while serving as President that we have the best evidence for Lincoln's involvement with Spiritualism. We have seen that he had at least some contact with mediums and Spiritualist hangers-on from the very beginning of his administration. However, beginning in 1862, the documentation for more serious involvement with mediums and the Washington coterie of Spiritualists is strong and it is not hard to see the reason for Lincoln's behavior.

In early 1862, both Willie and Tad Lincoln fell gravely ill with Typhoid Fever; Tad was near death's door for weeks while Willie died in February. Both Abraham and Mary were devastated by the loss, although each expressed their grief in their own way. Both Lincoln and his wife had visitations from their deceased son in the dead of the night.

It is from this period onward, to the end of the war, that the best evidence is most substantial for both Lincolns being heavily involved with mediums and Spiritualism. However, before looking at the evidence itself, it is necessary to look at the basic assumptions behind how historians have handled the evidence, since their long-held assumptions have led to distortions that are still prevalent today.

The assertion that President Lincoln had little or no involvement with séances and mediums is a position that dates back virtually to the time of Lincoln's demise. While there was a general awareness that paranormal events surrounded Lincoln's death at the time, there quickly arose a whole industry of hagiographers dedicated to turning Lincoln into a plaster saint. Lincoln's involvement with Spiritualism clearly did not square with the post-mortem conversion of him as an orthodox Protestant, and scholars, for various reasons, have more or less followed this line with little questioning until it became an unquestioned dogma.

The Lincoln War Cabinet, 1861. Was this a "team of rivals," as some historians assert, or a circle of Spiritualists? One publication said that Lincoln's connection to Spiritualism was the real cause of the war.

In recent decades, however, there has been some softening of attitudes on this subject by mainstream biographers of the 16th President. As an example, we may contrast Irving Stone's 1972 comments on the subject with David Herbert Donald's 1996 assessment.

Irving Stone, who did much to rehabilitate Mary Todd Lincoln's reputation, portrayed the Lincolns' involvement with séances as solely hers: "She allowed herself to be persuaded to attend a number of spiritualist meetings....she even permitted one of the more demanding spiritualists to hold a séance in the White House, a mistake in judgment which the President dressed her down."[125]

However, David Hebert Donald, writing twenty-four years later, has this assessment: "Perhaps as many as eight séances were held in the White House itself. Lincoln attended, but he was not convinced."[126]

Despite some concessions to the evidence, the inherited dogma remains very much in evidence regarding the Lincolns' involvement with this aspect of the paranormal presidency. For example, the well-respected website "Mr. Lincoln's White House," in its essay on the subject, labels the whole topic "Mary's Charlatans."[127]

While it is true that scholarly preconceptions on the subject have caused certain facts to be ignored or downgraded, it is also true that there were mediums in Washington during the 1860s who *were* accomplished frauds. The rapid growth of interest in Spiritualism in the 1850s, plus the fact that there was no way of separating legitimate adherents from crass opportunists, meant that a number of con artists made quite a healthy living off of Spiritualism. However, this does not negate the fact that there were also many sincere advocates who believed in what they were doing.

In addition to the Lauries' home in Georgetown, there were several other places where Spiritualists gathered to attend séances; the home of Thomas Gales Foster was one such place. There were also itinerant mediums such as Father Beeson, who packed the Odd Fellows Hall and was in communication with the deceased Judge Dean, a noted New York jurist and defender of fugitive slaves. All went well for the padre until he communicated a message from a dead colored man that African Americans occupied the chief seats in paradise, which did not sit well with his all-white audience.[128]

There was a whole parade of mediums in Washington during the war, many of whom claimed to hold séances for the President and Mrs. Lincoln. The claims of these different mediums varied widely in both veracity and accuracy. Some may well have been truthful, but simply lacked any corroboration; others were arrant knaves. Of all these, one medium's claims stand out, supported by other eyewitnesses and contemporary evidence: Henrietta Colburn.

Henrietta, generally known by her nickname "Nettie," did not come to the Capitol out of opportunism nor was she a "professional at her phony craft," as one historian avers.[129] Rather, it was the tides of war that drew her there and, she believed, the actions of the "congress of spirits," which directed her fate.

Nettie's family was from Connecticut, around the town of Bolton originally. By the outbreak of the Civil War, however, her family was residing in Hartford. When she was still young, her family had several experiences in their Bolton home that they believed were supernatural attempts to contact them by deceased family members. These early experiences led young Nettie to experiment with developing psychic powers.

Nettie's initial attempts at developing her psychic potential proved fruitless. However, Nettie and a friend continued to "sit" and eventually she was able to produce rapping sounds. Ultimately, she was able to sit and have the physical phenomena come to her at-will; the entity or entities also began to make sounds to communicate with her.

Henrietta's father was a staunch Republican and so naturally Nettie herself was also a supporter of their presidential candidate in 1856 — John C. Fremont. Yet, on the eve of the election, Nettie's hand seemed to be taken over by some outside force. Putting a pen in her hand, it scribbled out the word "Buchanan" — the opposing candidate. When Nettie's prediction came true on Election Day, her family needed no further convincing that she was indeed gifted.

While Nettie Colburn began her career as a medium with the traditional table-rapping, which is sometimes referred to as the "Spirit Telegraph," her prophetic pick of the correct presidential candidate was an example of what she called "mechanical writing" or, what is today referred to as, automatic writing.

As her psychic talents developed, however, Nettie evolved into what was called a "trance medium." Mesmerism had also been of substantial influence on the evolving Spiritualist movement and many, like Nettie, became very adept at self-induced hypnotic trances. Miss Colburn would become completely unconscious as some spirit seemingly would take control of her body and speak through her. Often the spirit taking possession of her would deliver sophisticated intellectual or political monologues in a manner far above the level of Nettie's own education and background. Others present at her séance would have to tell her what she had said.

When war broke out, the Colburn family, like other loyal citizens, heeded Lincoln's call and father and sons joined the Connecticut Volunteer Infantry. They marched off to war to defend Lincoln and the Capitol.

Meanwhile, although the spirits were telling Nettie to go to Washington to carry an important message to the President, she resisted their urgings. Nettie was well aware that in the male dominated world of Washington she would be regarded as crazy and her message ignored. However, at the beginning of November 1862, Nettie received two letters in the mail that would changer her mind — and set her on a collision course with destiny.

One letter was from her youngest brother, Amasa Colburn, who was currently serving as a private in the 16th Connecticut Infantry. He was sick, very sick, but the medical care he was receiving in the field was inadequate and he told her that unless he could be granted a furlough to recover at home, he feared he would die.

The other letter came from the Spiritualist Society of Baltimore, Maryland, asking her to give a series of lectures for the society there. They would pay her an honorarium to cover her expenses. In one stroke, Nettie not only had an urgent reason to visit the Capitol, but had also been given the means to do so. To Nettie, it seemed as if her spirit helpers were engineering her visit, virtually against her better judgment.

During her first week in Baltimore, Nettie made inquiries through the sympathetic Spiritualists there about any folk in Washington who might help her in her quest to obtain a furlough for her sick brother, wasting away in Alexandria, Virginia. They referred her to Thomas Gales Foster, a well known Spiritualist who had obtained a position in the War Department.

Armed with a letter of introduction, Nettie was warmly received by Foster and his family. The very next day she went to meet Assistant Secretary of War Tucker, Foster's superior. Although her Spiritualist connections did open doors for her in Washington, the Federal bureaucracy was mightier still and after several weeks battling official red tape Nettie had still not obtained her brother Amasa's much-needed furlough.

In between her struggles with Washington bureaucrats, Nettie attended séances at the Foster residence, where she met former congressman Daniel E. Somes, Judge Hoar of the Interior Department, and Cranston Laurie of the Post Office. It was in this manner that Nettie "agreeably filled" a number of evenings in Washington.

However, after several ups and downs in her quest to obtain a medical furlough for Amasa, by late December, Nettie was at her wit's end. Then one evening, as Nettie prepared to leave Washington empty-handed, Mr. Laurie showed up at the Foster's and asked if "the children" (Nettie and her friend Parthenia Hannum) had departed yet. Finding them still there, he told Nettie to come with him and promised if she did so she would succeed in obtaining her injured brother's much-needed leave.

As a footman in livery helped her into the elegant carriage, adorned with crimson satin cushions, Nettie had an inkling that perhaps she was not going to an ordinary séance at the Lauries. On her arrival, Nettie was astonished to be presented to Mrs. Lincoln.

Also present at this séance were congressman D.E. Somes; the Honorable Isaac Newton, head of the newly created Agricultural Department; and the Reverend John Pierpont (as in J. Pierpont-Morgan), a senior bureaucrat in the Treasury Department.

Mary had already been informed of the talents of the physical medium Mrs. Miller, but the Lauries also informed Mrs. Lincoln of Nettie's abilities and the First Lady had a desire to witness a trance medium. The Lauries, aware of Nettie's frustration, were not certain whether or not she had already left town, which was why the Presidential carriage had been dispatched post haste to the Foster residence.

Soon after arriving at the Laurie home, Nettie went into a trance that lasted an hour. Miss Colburn herself remained unaware of what she said during that time, but was told afterwards that she had "addressed Mrs. Lincoln...with great clearness and force upon matters of state." Informed of the plight of Nettie's brother, Mrs. Lincoln promised to put in a word on his behalf with her husband. Even the mighty Washington bureaucracy could not resist Mary Lincoln's whim of iron when put to the test.

Within days, Amasa Colburn was headed home on medical leave. Once away from the intransigence of the military red tape of the Army of the Potomac, the private of Company F, 16th Connecticut Volunteer Infantry, eventually received a discharge, "with disability," on August 3, 1863.[130]

Nettie, however, stayed in the Capitol; for one thing Mary Todd Lincoln insisted on it. The First Lady also prevailed on the venerable Isaac Newton to find a spot for her and her friend in the Agricultural Department, so she might have a means of support while in the Capitol conducting séances for the Lincolns and others.[131]

The day after her brother's departure for Hartford, Nettie received a note from the First Lady, inviting her to the White House that very evening. Accompanied by the Lauries, Nettie was ushered into the Red Parlor (today the Red Room) of the White House. After being introduced to a few other guests, the evening began with Mrs. Miller playing on the parlor's grand piano. The parlor entertainment soon turned supernatural, however; the legs of the grand piano began rising and falling in tune to the music.

All at once, the music ceased. The President stood upon the threshold to the Red Parlor. Mr. and Mrs. Laurie were presented first, then Mrs. Miller. Finally Nettie was led forward and presented to the President. "He stood before me, tall and kindly, with a smile on his face," Nettie tells us.

Dropping his hand upon her head, Lincoln says in a humorous tone, "So this is our 'little Nettie' is it…that we have heard so much about?" Although 21 years old, Nettie is very petite and, with the tall President of the United States towering over her, Nettie feels like a little school girl. She smiles and simply says, "Yes, sir."

Leading her over to an Ottoman, Lincoln sits in the chair next to her and begins asking her about her mediumship. After a few minutes of conversation, it is suggested that the persons present form a circle for a séance. Lincoln asks, "Well, how do you do it?" looking at Nettie as he speaks. Mrs. Laurie comes to the rescue, saying that they are accustomed to sitting in a circle and joining hands.

No sooner does Mrs. Laurie utter the words than Lincoln observes, "I do not think it will be necessary in this instance," for, as he is speaking, Nettie loses all consciousness of her surroundings and "passes under control."

For more than an hour, the unconscious young lady holds forth on various subjects to the President, mostly on matters of state. Miss Colburn herself is oblivious of all this and only knows what others tell her later about it.

Although her controlling spirit holds forth on many issues to Lincoln, it isn't until the spirit inhabiting her starts discussing the Emancipation Proclamation that the other people in the room make any sense of the "spirit lecture." Channeling a masculine entity (or so it seems), Nettie exhorted Lincoln "not to delay its enforcement as a law beyond the opening of the year." Nettie's controlling spirit goes on to tell Lincoln that "it is to be the crowning event of [your] administration and life."

At the same time, the President is warned to "in no wise heed such counsel" to defer the enforcement of the Proclamation," but "to stand firm to [your] convictions." All those present are impressed both by Nettie's force of language and "majesty of the utterance."[132]

As Nettie regains consciousness, she is at first disoriented. Next to her Lincoln also seems to be "shaking off his spell." Apparently, Nettie is not the only one to have entered into a trance.

Another guest present pointed out the spirit's "peculiar method of address" to Lincoln as he is gazing up at a portrait of Daniel Webster. Lincoln's response implies that he, too, thinks the spirit's "singular" mode of speech was that of the famed New England orator's.

In light of Daniel Webster's forceful exhortation (by way of

Caleb B. Smith, Secretary of the Interior. Secretary Smith acted as a go-between for Spiritualists with Lincoln.

John W. Forney, Carte de Visite. Well-known Washington newspaper editor and strong supporter of the Lincoln administration, Forney also had strong ties to the Washington Spiritualist circles.

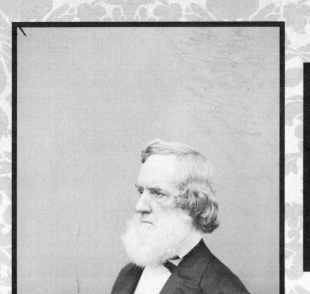

Gideon Welles, Secretary of the Navy. Besides being an able administrator, Welles was a confirmed Spiritualist. His wife, Mary, was a close friend of the First Lady. Both Mr. and Mrs. Welles, like the Lincolns, had lost young children to disease and, like the Lincolns, they attended séances to get in touch with their deceased child.

S. P. Chase, Secretary of the Treasury. Although he thought himself more fit to be President than Lincoln, he helped the President finance the war. Chase was also a militant Abolitionist and like many Abolitionists was also a Spiritualist. His wife was described as the "one of the best mediums in Ohio."

Edwin Stanton, Secretary of War. Although he was a hard-headed lawyer and politician, Stanton is known to have frequented séances.

William Seward, Secretary of State. Like others in the cabinet, Seward is known to have attended séances during the war.

Nettie), Congressman Somes asks Lincoln rather pointedly whether he is in fact under pressure to put off making the preliminary Emancipation Proclamation final. Lincoln tells Somes, "It is taking all my nerve and strength to withstand such pressure."[133]

With hindsight, history views the Emancipation Proclamation as a great deed that won universal acclaim. In truth, while progressive elements throughout the North hailed the declaration, there were many others who roundly condemned it. To some, the three months delay between the preliminary declaration in September and official issuance in January was seen by some as an opportunity to stop the declaration or substantially water it down.[134]

While some Spiritualists claimed that Nettie Colburn's spirit talk persuaded Lincoln to issue the Emancipation Proclamation, Nettie herself never made that claim; that particular assertion was based on the faulty recollections of an eyewitness to the December séance — Colonel Kase.

As we've seen, Lincoln had already issued the preliminary Proclamation based on divine intervention, so her exhortation on that count was unnecessary. However, Nettie as Daniel Webster did serve as a welcome confirmation from beyond that the President had made the right decision and her words encouraged him to stay the course. Lincoln had already obtained the approval of Providence, it helped to also have the approval of the "congress of spirits."

Nettie was not the only voice in the Spiritualist camp exhorting Lincoln to stay the course. Inside and outside the administration, Lincoln's Spiritualist friends and allies — also largely Abolitionists — provided advice and political support.

Even within Lincoln's own cabinet there were members who had participated in séances and could be counted in the Spiritualist camp. The cabinet member with the strongest credentials in this regard was Gideon Welles, the Secretary of the Navy, and his wife. The Welles' interest in séances began in much the same way as the Lincolns did during the war.

In 1854, in the wake of his daughter Anna Jane's death, Gideon Welles began attending séances at the suggestion of a newspaper associate. His wife also participated in sessions to contact their deceased daughter.[135]

Gideon Welles had begun his political career as a Jacksonian Democrat and was also a New England newspaper editor. However, more and more Welles' Free Soil politics encountered hostility within his own party and earned him a welcome home in the new Republican Party. Welles helped first with the Fremont presidential campaign in 1856 and then with Lincoln's in 1860. His efforts on behalf of Lincoln in the northeast earned him a spot in the Lincoln cabinet — the only New Englander appointed to a cabinet level post.

Welles soon earned Lincoln's trust through his honesty and his effectiveness in creating a modern navy from scratch. Of equal importance,

Welles' wife, Mary Jane, managed to attain the daunting goal of earning Mrs. Lincoln's trust and friendship. When William and Tad fell ill, Mary Welles actually moved into the White House to help the First Lady and provide emotional support.

It has been claimed that Mrs. Lincoln's "modiste" (dressmaker), Elizabeth Keckley, was the one who first suggested to Mary Lincoln that she attend a séance to get back in touch with her son Willie. However, it has been pointed out that while Negroes had a very well established occult tradition of their own; séances seemed to have been more popular among Whites interested in the paranormal and Miss Keckley would more likely have referred the First Lady to the plentiful Negro seers in the Washington area.[136]

Given the close relationship between Mary Welles and Mary Lincoln, as well as their loss of a child in common, the Welles' were far more likely to have directed the Lincolns in that direction...not that they needed much pushing.

Inside the cabinet, there were others who attended séances during the war years, although one might quibble whether as mere dabblers or more dedicated participants. We have already seen that Interior Secretary Caleb B. Smith likely had a relationship with Spiritualism; likewise both Edwin Stanton and Salmon P. Chase are known to have attended séances. Certainly, the venerable Isaac Newton of the new Agricultural Department was an active enthusiast. Other bureaucrats in the War Department,

such as Assistant Secretary of War Tucker, were also at least sympathetic to the movement.

Within the Treasury Department, John Pierpont, who held "a valuable post," was an avid Spiritualist. He had given up his position as pastor of the Hollis Street Church in Boston to devote himself to the movement; a poet and writer, as well as a social activist and mystic, he "had the absolute confidence of Mr. and Mrs. Lincoln."[137] Pierpont's son composed the popular Christmas Carol "Jingle Bells" while his grandson was none other than famed financier J. Pierpont Morgan.

If we cast the net farther, to Capitol Hill, we find even larger numbers of Spiritualists and their supporters. We have already seen that former congressman and powerful patent lawyer Daniel Somes was certainly in the Spiritualist camp.

Senator Benjamin Wade, of Ohio, was an unabashed Spiritualist and militant Abolitionist; however, he also personally disliked Lincoln, whom he thought too moderate. According to one contemporary, "Mr. Wade's wife is said to be one of the best mediums in Ohio."[138]

Charles Sumner, another Radical Republican, was at least open to the Spiritualist constituency, as he had co-sponsored a piece of legislation in 1854 for the Federal government to officially investigate Spiritualism's claims.

Senator Edwin D. Morgan acted as go-between for a noted New York Spiritualist and the President. One may assume that he was at least a "fellow traveler," if not a participant in séances.

Longtime congressman J.J. Giddings was a close political ally of Senator Wade and, like Wade, was a fierce Abolitionist and confirmed Spiritualist, as well as an activist for other progressive causes. Irritations with Giddings' militancy may have been the motive behind Lincoln appointing him Consul to Canada — one way, at least, to remove him from the immediate Washington scene.

The Lincolns' participation in séances, whatever their motivation, did not go unnoticed by either the general press or the President's political enemies. In 1863, one particularly nasty screed by a "Citizen of Ohio" (actually a lawyer from Chicago) used this fact as a weapon against the Lincoln Administration. In actual fact, the author of this diatribe was himself a Spiritualist; his real source of hatred of all things Lincoln was his use of force to suppress the Rebellion and his issuing of the Emancipation Proclamation. He described Lincoln as "a spiritualist of the abolitionist school" whom he claims was "directing the war under direction of spirit rappings."[139]

The *Baltimore Republican*, despite the paper's name, was apparently an anti-Lincoln outlet: its article "A New Key to Our Troubles," which tells us "upon unquestionable authority that Mr. Lincoln is a convert to the doctrine of spiritual rappings, manifestations, and rapport theories." It cites various other political associates known to be Spiritualists, such as Robert Dale Owens, Joshua Giddings, and "Phillips (Wendell Phillips) and all the atheistical club of New England" as corroboration. One paper that reprinted the article also added that "a prominent state official from Kentucky" stated to the reporter that "the President had given himself into the hands of dreams and theorists, and that he regarded him as insane."[140]

Although the proclamation itself was largely symbolic, it put the world on notice that slavery's days were limited. As soon as the Secession Crisis was over, it was obvious that all slaves would be free in fact as well as theory. Lincoln's and liberty's enemies saw in Spiritualism a weapon to use against the President.

Doubtless there were still others in the Lincoln Administration who were also interested in the movement, but who were less willing to suffer public humiliation and kept their "spirit-rapping" more discreet.

Nettie Colburn was not the only medium whom the Lincolns consulted during this same period. We learn from Congressman Orville Browning that the First Lady attended a New Year's Eve séance along with Isaac Newton, which could not have been much more than a week after the White House séance with Miss Colburn.[141]

Nettie's next recorded meeting with the Lincolns was on February 5, 1863, once again at the Laurie residence. As before, Nettie went into a trance and was oblivious to the proceedings, but others present informed her much of what she said and we also have another eyewitness who left a written account — several in fact.[142]

For this outing to the inner realm, the late Daniel Webster was not present, but one of Nettie's favorite familiars, "old Dr. Bamford" was. Bamford was quite the favorite with the President. "His quaint dialect, old-fashioned methods of expression, straightforwardness... with fearlessness," found a positive audience in Lincoln.

Dr. Bamford had informed Lincoln in no uncertain terms of the serious condition of the Army of the Potomac, especially since General Hooker had assumed command. Although McClellan had singularly failed to defeat the Rebels, he had been a favorite among the soldiers; Hooker was equally unable to defeat the enemy, but at a much higher cost of life. The spirited doctor urged Lincoln to visit the front in person; not to confer with the officers of the army, but to mingle with the men.

"Show yourself to be what you are," Bamford said. "The Father of the People...it will unite the soldiers as one man, unite them to you in bands of steel."

Lincoln replied, "It shall be done."

Dr. Bamford also reassured Lincoln that he would indeed be re-elected when he ran again.

It was at this February séance that Belle Miller gave her famous demonstration as a "moving medium." Mrs. Miller was an accomplished pianist and her music alone was worth the visit to Lincoln, but the good lady had wider talents.

As she sat at the three-cornered grand piano serenading the audience, the legs of the piano began to "rise and fall" in tune to the rhythm of the music.

Cranston Laurie suggested a "test" for Mrs. Miller. She would stand at arm's length from the keyboard as she played it, to demonstrate that there was no sort of manipulation involved in the levitation. The President then placed his hand underneath the piano to assure himself there was no mechanical agency involved.

Next, Belle put her left hand on his, as further proof that no strength or pressure was being used to lift the piano. The piano rose and fell several times in this position.

"With a quaint smile," Lincoln said, "I think we can hold down this instrument," whereupon he hopped on the grand piano, his long legs dangling over the side. Next Daniel Somes, Colonel Kase, and an unnamed army major also joined the President atop the piano. Despite the added weight, the piano continued to wobble and buck. As Colonel Kase tells us, "The piano jumped so violently and shook us up so roughly that we were thankful to get off it."

All in all, the February 5th séance was convincing proof to all present that Miss Colburn and Mrs. Miller were genuine and possessed of extraordinary gifts. Nettie says that Lincoln confidentially verified what she had said while unconscious; many were facts unknown to anyone outside the cabinet — and some facts known only to Lincoln himself.

Nettie's advice to visit the troops was heeded and, while the effects of her lecture were not quite immediate as she assumed, Lincoln's visit to the front did have a salutary effect on morale.

Throughout 1863 and 1864, Miss Colburn continued attending séances, both with the Lincolns and without them in Washington. In the fall of 1864, Nettie left the Capitol to go on a speaking tour in New England, which, for all intents and purposes, was a campaign tour for the President.[143] Throughout all this, Nettie gained no material benefit from her sittings for the Lincolns, although she did at times seek favors on behalf of others.

In the fall of 1863, for example, Nettie and a Washington friend, Mrs. Cosby, visited the President. Curiously, she solicited a letter of introduction from the President's old friend, Joshua Speed. As Nettie had been meeting with both Lincolns for nearly a year, the October 26th letter from Speed would seem anachronistic.[144]

However, in her memoirs, Nettie explains that it was at the behest of her friend Anna Cosby. Her husband had been US Consul to Venice, but had been relieved from his post on rumor that he had been associating with Confederate agents, so Nettie's friend thought it wise if Lincoln's old friend wrote the note. Speed was visiting Washington and Nettie's best friend, Parthenia Hannum, had conducted a séance for him, where Speed's deceased servant got back in touch with his old master.[145]

While the boon that Nettie sought for a third party was granted, what is most interesting about the incident is the tone of Speed's letter. Speed and Lincoln had been roommates in their bachelor days and best friends — one escapee from the Kinsey Institute has even claimed they were friends "with benefits." At any rate, Speed describes the two ladies as "mediums and believers in the spirits" and expresses his opinion that meeting them "will I am sure be some relief from the tedious round of office seekers," for his friend. The letter assumes Lincoln's familiarity with mediums and Spiritualism and that he would welcome the two ladies as such. The letter not only verifies Mrs. Maynard's account, but it also corroborates the fact of Lincoln's positive attitude towards Spiritualism in general.

Nettie continued to sit for both the President and the First Lady off and on throughout the war, until February 1865, when family matters summoned her home. Throughout this time, though, there were other mediums that the President and his wife consulted, not just those associated with the Lauries. Nettie herself mentions Charles Foster and Charles Colchester.

Foster — "Salem's Seer" — had an interesting way of communicating with his spirits. Rather than rapping on a table, the entities (if such they were) chose to communicate with him by blazing their names or initials on his bare skin, usually the forearm. Foster repeated the feat often and allowed such close inspection that it precluded any fakery. Doubtless Mr. Foster could have given Padre Pio a run for the money.[146]

Colchester, who styled himself Lord Colchester, definitely earned the epithet of being one of "Mary's Charlatans," although he apparently performed for both Lincolns. Charles J. Colchester's nobility was self-anointed, but his elaborate séances — conducted in darkened rooms with all sorts of objects floating in the air — apparently caught the fancy of the First Lady. During the winter of 1864-65, he staged his shows for the Lincolns, including at least one séance at the Soldier's Home, which the Lincolns used as a family retreat when the pressure of Washington politics and society became too pressing.

The President was less impressed than his wife by the scratching sounds and the floating trumpets of Colchester and asked Dr. Joseph Henry, the head of the Smithsonian, to conduct an objective evaluation of Colchester's psychic abilities. While Henry could not prove Colchester a phony, he felt the sounds in the room emanated from the medium himself and not from any spirits.[147]

It was up to journalist Noah Brooks, a friend of both the President's and Mrs. Lincoln's, to expose Colchester. Brooks, on his own initiative, attended a Colchester séance at a private residence where an admission fee was charged. The séance, held in the dark, included all the bells and whistles, plus a banjo, drums, and an assortment of other floating paraphernalia. In the midst of the performance, Brooks loosened his hands from his neighbors around the tale and, reaching up into the dark, grabbed Colchester in mid-drumbeat. Brooks, on his own authority, threatened Colchester with a stretch in the Old Capitol prison if he should ever bother the First Family again.[148]

Warren Chase, the Midwest politician, ran into Colchester in January 1865. At that time, the shameless Colchester confided that "he often cheated the fools, as he could easily do it, but never deceived the honest and intelligent inquirers."[149] When last heard from, Colchester had been convicted of "jugglery" without a license.[150]

Again, these mediums were not the only ones who graced the Lincolns presence during the rest of the war. There seems to have been a whole parade of them who were consulted by one or the other. Some of them were well known while others apparently were obscure, with little save their names. They were also a mixed lot; some were sincere while others were of equally dubious character as Colchester.

One of the better documented séances that the President attended occurred in April 1863. Again, the séance took place in the "Crimson Room" (The Red Room) of the White House, conducted by a gentleman named Charles E. Shockle. We know quite a bit about this session through the good offices of a correspondent for the *Boston Gazette*, Prior Melton, who was specially invited to attend.[151]

Among those present for the séance at the White House besides Mr. Lincoln were Secretary of the Navy Welles and Secretary of War Stanton, as well as a gentleman from New York and Philadelphia who apparently did not wish to be identified by name. The participants seated themselves in a circle in the Crimson Room around 8 p.m., but shortly after the session began the President was called away on business.

Apparently, the President's absence upset the spirits in the room, as they pinched Stanton's ear and twitched Welles' beard. Although Lincoln soon returned to the session, "it was some time before harmony was restored," as the pranks played on the Secretaries caused such mirth that the medium found conditions "unpropitious." There were other physical demonstrations as well: tables moved and a picture of Henry Clay on the wall began to sway back and forth. When a loud rapping was heard beneath Lincoln's feet, Shockle said that an Indian spirit wished to communicate.

"Well, sir," said Lincoln, "I should be happy to hear what his Indian majesty has to say. We have recently had a visitation from our red brethren and it was the only delegation, black, white, or blue which did not volunteer some advice about the conduct of the war."

Next, the medium called for pen and paper and covered them with a handkerchief. After a moment or two, a knock was heard and the objects were uncovered — a written message from beyond was on the paper, signed by Henry Knox, who had been President Washington's Secretary of War.

Lincoln asked the spirit of Knox if he had any war advice for Stanton. Apparently Knox consulted a committee of famous spirits, each of whom offered suggestions. Heavy raps were then heard; "the alphabet" was called for and the spirit present directed its comments at Welles, who gave a noncommittal reply to the spirit and stroked his beard. Lincoln asked the spirits how to catch the Confederate raider the *C.S.S. Alabama*, which was bedeviling Union merchant ships at the time. At this, the room, where the lights had already been dimmed, went dark and a series of pictures began to appear on the mirror over the mantle-piece illustrating the *Alabama* and its piratical career. The final picture showed it seized by the English.

Finally, Lincoln asked Shockle to summon his old rival Stephen Douglas for advice. On cue, the spirit of the deceased Douglas took over the medium and declaimed for awhile on how to win the war. After that, the medium seemed worn out and Lincoln thought it best to "adjourn the dance" and the séance ended.

This séance was widely publicized; not just in Boston and New York, but throughout the Midwest and far West newspapers picked it up and ran with the story. The *New York Herald's* version of this article adds the fact that John W. Forney, the editor of the *Washington Courier* was also present. This séance was very much a media event.

As well known as this particular séance was, the curious fact is that both the cynics and the Spiritualists have labeled it a fabrication — that some reporter invented the story out of thin air. Yet, on the face of it, there is nothing about the reported séance to indicate the story was a hoax. The name "Shockle" is not familiar to students of Spiritualism, it is said; of course the fact that mediums were almost literally popping up on every street corner in those days means that the gentleman's psychic abilities may merely have been of recent manufacture. Although Melton did not get a by-line on the original printing of the story, he later ran it in a Spiritualist journal with his name. He was active in Boston Spiritualist circles apparently, as well as writing pieces for the *Gazette*.[152]

The White House never denied the newspaper report and the fact that it had such widespread currency would surely have elicited a denial if the story were a complete fabrication. Insofar as the debunkers and upholders of the Lincoln orthodoxy are concerned, their accusations simply don't hold water. As to the later Spiritualist's criticism of the story, a close reading of the article illuminates why they might deny one of their own. The tone of the article — especially of Lincoln's attitude towards the proceedings — is decidedly jocular. Moreover, there is no mention of emancipation or arming the slaves, just prosecuting the war. While Lincoln is portrayed as an active participant, he is less a devoted spirit-rapper and more the bemused spectator. The purpose of the séance seemed more for entertainment than enlightenment.

The *New York Herald's* mention of the *Washington Courier* editor Forney being also present makes one suspicious that something more than either a hoax or fabrication is going on here. This was no secret conclave, but an event intended to be widely publicized.

Mitch Horowitz, who has investigated some of the more esoteric aspects of American history, has a theory about this particular séance and its true purpose. Although the majority of northern Spiritualists were solidly behind Lincoln and welcomed the President and his wife's participation in séances, there were many others in the North who were uneasy over reports of the President consorting with mediums. We have seen that his political enemies had already used this fact to try to undermine his

administration and the war effort.

By the spring of 1863, the fact that Lincoln had attended séances was well known nationally; there was no point in trying to deny it. What Mitch Horowitz theorizes is that the Shockle article was a conscious attempt by the Lincoln administration and their friends in journalism to put a different "spin" on that fact. No, the President is not controlled by some occult conspiracy of Spiritualists... Yes, the President attends séances, but it is merely a diversion from the heavy weight of his war duties and Old Abe by no means takes it seriously. This, in effect, is the gist of the Shockle article that Lincoln's allies in the press distributed so far and wide.[153] If this theory is correct, then the issue of whether Charles Schockle was a genuine medium or not is irrelevant. The article certainly served its purpose — and Lincoln continued to frequent mediums.

If this, in fact, was the administration's goal in promoting the story of the Shockle séance at the White House, it couldn't have been a more brilliant piece of political maneuvering. On the one hand it mollified Republican supporters who were hostile to the Spiritualist movement and uneasy with the notion of Lincoln being one of their numbers. It also undermined the Copperheads who had tried to portray Lincoln as a mere pawn in the hands of demonic forces. At the same time, by not overtly denying that Lincoln attended séances, it also did not offend those in the Republican ranks who believed in the movement.

After Lincoln's death, innumerable articles came out in the press with their headlines asking, "Was Lincoln a Spiritualist?" Nettie Colburn Maynard (Nettie had married a lieutenant in her father's regiment) posed that question as the title of her memoirs, and it is still being asked and answered in both the positive and negative to this day. It behooves us, then, to also tackle the issue: was Lincoln a Spiritualist, really?

After weighing all the evidence, we must answer the question with a definitive...it depends. If by Spiritualist, one means that Lincoln was a devoted adherent, willing to accept unquestioningly every table-tipping, spirit rapping, smooth talking, self-anointed seer that passed before his purview, then the answer is no...he was not. If, however, one accepts that Lincoln's inquiring mind, his mystic inclinations, and his innate curiosity led him to investigate Spiritualism with an open mind, then the answer would be yes.

Bear in mind, Albert Einstein, who, like Lincoln in his youth, did not believe in life after death, also attended a séance. Einstein was open-minded enough to investigate the possibility, even if he remained unconvinced.[154]

Even by the testimony of some Spiritualists, it is clear that Lincoln's attitude towards mediums, séances, and contacting the dead was nuanced. Colonel Bundy, editor of the Chicago Spiritualist periodical The *Religio-Philosophical Journal*, weighed in on the issue, saying of Lincoln "while it is quite possible that he received advice from the spirit world, it is also certain that he never blindly followed it. It would have to conform to his own better judgment before being adopted."[155]

Mrs. Maynard, whose eyewitness testimony is all the more credible for her circumspection regarding the claims she made for her séances with the President, was also circumspect when it came to claiming Lincoln as a convert to Spiritualism: "No claim is made that all persons named in connection with my mediumistic experiences in the White House at Washington, or elsewhere in the several circles of that city, were Spiritualists."[156]

Nonetheless, during the war, many in Washington and elsewhere involved in the Spiritualist movement believed Lincoln was at least a sympathetic observer if not one of them. In forwarding two of his books on Spiritualism to Lincoln in June 1863, Judge John W. Edwards of New York said, "Amid my consideration of that subject I was assured...that we should have a Spiritualist as a President. When that would be I was not told. Keeping that in view, I have heard and read in various ways, without surprize that you, Sir, are so far interested in the subject, as to have entered upon its investigation."[157]

Abraham Lincoln certainly attended numerous séances on repeated occasions all through the war. Those held in the White House are reported to have taken place in the Red Room, with the Lauries' home in Georgetown another popular location; at least one séance was also held at the Soldier's Home, a discreet retreat located on the outskirts of town. Lincoln's repeated attendance at these meetings indicates a more than passing interest in the subject.

As to Lincoln's motives for participating in the séances, these seem to be mixed. Although a skeptic by training, Lincoln was curious by nature and superstitious by his upbringing and culture. His initial interest in Spiritualism seems to date back to well before the war and did not involve Mary at all. However, the death of his son Willie was a transformative event, both for Lincoln and his wife. While Abraham and Mary grieved for Willie in different ways, both were severely affected by his death and both had nighttime visitations of their son after his death, which is not an uncommon occurrence even today. That they should turn to mediums to get in touch with their dead son would be understandable — and an increasingly common occurrence as the Civil War wore on and battlefield fatalities mounted.

Another part of Lincoln's — and Mary's — motivation for attending the séances was as a diversion from the daily stresses of wartime Washington. There had always been an entertainment element to a séance and we know that Lincoln was fond of theater. Indeed, in the latter part of the nineteenth century, the Spiritualist movement was attacked with vengeance by stage magicians like Houdini, in large part because they saw it as unwanted theatrical competition that stole audiences away from them.

We have seen that there was also a definite political aspect to the Spiritualist movement as well. There were many in the Lincoln Administration who had at least attended séances; Congress, too, had its coterie of Spiritualist adherents. We know that some in the Lincoln cabinet were serious about their involvement with the movement; others in the administration may have simply found it politic to play along and stay in the President's and First Lady's good graces — the latter of which certainly seems to have been General Daniel Sickles' motivation in attending the White House séances.

How many bureaucrats and politicians associated with Lincoln and his administration were dedicated Spiritualists we shall never know precisely, though we do know that they were sufficiently numerous to attract negative public attention and to be used by those who hated Lincoln, his wartime policies, and his support of Negro rights as a weapon against him. However, the Copperhead calumnies that asserted that Lincoln took his marching orders from the spirit world or a Spiritualist cabal may well have had a grain of truth to it. It may not so much have been that Lincoln was manipulated by the Spiritualists, as that he was able to manipulate them to further his political ends.

The confluence of Spiritualism with other progressive movements, such as Abolitionism, and the influential make-up of its membership in the North were a potentially powerful network of supporters. That Lincoln already held many beliefs in common with such folk made such an alliance as logical as it was irresistible.

In the course of his efforts to save the Union and emancipate the slaves, Lincoln made use of whatever political traction he could obtain, from whatever faction he could use. Thus, to Protestant ministers, Lincoln was a devout Christian; to German and Irish immigrant groups, he was their benefactor and friend. If Lincoln was not completely in the Spiritualist camp intellectually, they certainly were in his.

Chapter 16

A Strangely Annoying Dream....

"'Who is dead in the White House?' I demanded of one of the soldiers.
'The President,' was his answer; 'he was killed by an assassin!'"

— *Abraham Lincoln, 1865*

"Abraham's Dream!" Lincoln's belief in prophetic dreams and omens was no secret in his own day, as this political cartoon demonstrates.

During the latter part of March, Lincoln had taken ship aboard the steamboat *River Queen* to go down the Potomac to City Point, Virginia, the massive supply base established to support Grant's siege of Richmond and Petersburg. The end was fast approaching for the Confederacy and Lincoln wished to be there for the finale. A few days afterward, his wife Mary also joined him at City Point.

One day early in April 1865, while the couple were aboard the *River Queen*, Mary Todd Lincoln noticed her husband was in a particularly "melancholy, meditative mood." The silence was deafening. Mary, concerned, tried to stir her husband out of his somber mood. Something was deeply troubling Abe and, like many wives, Mary simply would not rest till she had pried the truth out of him.

At length, Lincoln responded, although at first it seemed almost as though he were in a trance, talking in slow measured tones. Lincoln rambled on with regard to the subject of dreams, and how much the Bible mentions them. No less than sixteen passages in the Old Testament and at least four in the New Testament, he told her, refer to dreams as messages from God — not to mention many other passages referring to visions. Lincoln had obviously been making a study of the subject.

"If we believe the Bible," Lincoln told wife and friends, "we must accept the fact that in the old days God and the angels came to men in their sleep and made themselves known in dreams." By way of disclaimer, however, Lincoln added, "Nowadays dreams are regarded as very foolish, and are seldom told, except by old women and young men and maidens in love."

Mary, noting Abe's solemn visage as he told her all this, asked pointedly, "Do *you* believe in dreams?" As he often did, Abe prefaced his response with a disclaimer, replying, "I can't say I do." Then, dropping the other shoe, Lincoln said, "but I had one the other night which has haunted me ever since."

Lincoln went on to tell Mary how, after his disturbing dream, upon waking he had turned to the Bible and, strangely, no matter what page he opened, he seemed to encounter a passage describing a dream or vision of some sort — passages, he said, "strangely in keeping with my own thought."

Lincoln looked so somber as he said this that Mary burst out, "You frighten me! What is the matter?"

Realizing that he was upsetting his wife, Lincoln once again tried to downplay his dream, but Mary's curiosity was now inflamed and, while "bravely disclaiming" any belief in dreams herself, Mary pressed Abe to tell her the dream that had affected him so much. The others present in the ship's stateroom also urged Lincoln to describe it, so, after having roused their interest, Lincoln began:

"About ten days ago...I retired very late. I had been up waiting for important dispatches from the front. I could not have been long in bed when I fell into a slumber, for I was weary. I soon began to dream.

"There seemed to be a death-like stillness about me. Then I heard subdued sobs, as if a number of people were weeping. I thought I left my bed and wandered downstairs. There the silence was broken by the same pitiful sobbing, but the mourners were invisible.

"I went from room to room; no living person was in sight, but the same mournful sounds of distress met me as I passed along. It was light in all the rooms; every object was familiar to me; but where were all the people who were grieving as if their hearts would break? I was puzzled and alarmed. What could be the meaning of all this?

"Determined to find the cause of a state of things so mysterious

and so shocking, I kept on until I arrived at the East Room, which I entered. There I met with a sickening surprise. Before me was a catafalque, on which rested a corpse wrapped in funeral vestments. Around it were stationed soldiers who were acting as guards; and there was a throng of people, some gazing mournfully upon the corpse, whose face was covered, others weeping pitifully.

"Who is dead in the White House? I demanded of one of the soldiers.

"'The President,' was his answer; 'He was killed by an assassin!'

"Then came a loud burst of grief from the crowd, which awoke me from my dream. I slept no more that night; and although it was only a dream, I have been strangely annoyed by it ever since."

Throughout the whole recital of his fatal dream, Lincoln's countenance was grave and gloomy — at times he was visibly pale — but also perfectly calm.

"That is horrid!" Mary exclaimed. "I wish you had not told it. I am glad I don't believe in dreams, or I should be in terror from this time forth."

Seeking to soothe his wife's fears, Lincoln said, "Well, it is only a dream, Mary. Let us say no more about it, and try to forget it."

Despite their mutual denial, both Lincolns were obviously quite disturbed by the incident, more so than by any of his other many previous dreams, visions, and presentiments. It would only be but a short span of days before this presentiment of Lincoln's came true with deadly accuracy.

On the night of April 14th, after the fatal attack on Lincoln, recalling this incident, the first words Mary Lincoln uttered were, "His dream was prophetic!"[158]

Chapter 17

Of a Ship Sailing Rapidly....

Here Captain! dear father!
This arm beneath your head!
It is some dream that on the deck,
You've fallen cold and dead.

— *Walt Whitman*

Walt Whitman, by Mathew Brady. One of America's greatest poets, he worked as a volunteer in Union hospitals during the war. Whitman's most famous poem, "Oh Captain, My Captain!" was based on Lincoln's last — and best known — prophetic dream of his own demise.

On April 13, 1865, only a few weeks after his terrifying dream of a funeral in the White House, Lincoln experienced yet another portentous dream. This one proved to be a familiar friend, however; one reassuring rather than disturbing to the President... although it, too, proved to be the final warning of what was to be.

The next morning, April 14th, the normal Friday cabinet meeting was held in the White House. This Friday's meeting, however, was anything but normal; it proved to be one of the most important sessions of the war. In contrast to many such prior gatherings earlier in the war, this cabinet meeting was very much an upbeat affair.

Lee had surrendered to Grant on the 9th; General Anderson, who had surrendered Fort Sumter four years before, had just raised Old Glory over that same battered fort in Charleston harbor; and news was expected any time from General Sherman, whose forces at that very moment were running the last major Confederate force — General Johnston's Army of Tennessee — to ground in North Carolina.

General Grant attended the meeting in person, to give the cabinet a first-hand account of Lee's surrender. The meeting had been scheduled to start at 9 a.m., but had been postponed to 11 a.m. As it turned out, the official start of the session was delayed still further, as Secretary of War Stanton was running late; the telegraph was in his department's offices and, likely, he was hoping to announce Johnston's surrender himself at the meeting.

While waiting on Stanton, they made small talk before the proceedings began in earnest:

> ❋ **GENERAL GRANT**: *"I am hourly expecting word from General Sherman.*

> ❋ **PRESIDENT LINCOLN**: *It will, no doubt, come soon, and come favorable, for I had the usual dream last night. Before every great national event I have always had the same dream. Generally the news has been favorable which succeeded this dream, and the dream itself is always the same.*

> ❋ **SECRETARY OF NAVY GIDEON WELLES**: *What could this remarkable dream be, Mr. President?*

> ❋ **PRESIDENT LINCOLN**: *It relates to your element, Mr. Welles — the water. I seem to be in some singular, indescribable vessel, and I am moving with great rapidity toward an indefinite shore. I have had this dream preceding the surrender of Fort Sumter, the Battles of Bull Run, Antietam, Gettysburg, Stone's River, Vicksburg, Wilmington, and...*

> ❋ **GENERAL GRANT (INTERRUPTING)**: *Stone's River was certainly no victory; I know of no great results which followed from it. A few more such fights would have ruined us!*

> ❋ **PRESIDENT LINCOLN (LOOKING AT GRANT CURIOUSLY AND INQUIRINGLY)**: *We may differ on that point, General; at all events, my dream preceded it. I had this strange dream again last night, and we shall, judging from the past, have great news very soon. I think it must be from Sherman. My thoughts are in that direction, as are most of yours."*[159]

They say that no man knows the hour of his dying, not even, apparently, one gifted with psychic abilities. According to Mary Lincoln, the often melancholy President was unusually cheerful that day. After the cabinet meeting, Abe and Mary went for a carriage ride in the afternoon and, during the ride, Mary commented on his jovial mood.

"And well I may feel so, Mary; for I consider this day the war has come to a close," he told her. Although news from Sherman still had not yet arrived, Lincoln had assumed his "usual dream" was a presentiment of victory — and not a presentiment of his own death.[160]

Likewise, from a brief conversation with a friend, it is clear that Lincoln had also dismissed the seemingly clear warning of a wake in the White House by rationalizing that it referred to someone else. "Don't you see how it will turn out?" he told Ward Lamon. "In this dream it was not me, but some other fellow that was killed. It seems that this ghostly assassin tried his hand on someone else."[161]

Lincoln may simply have been trying to allay concerns by a close and devoted friend about yet another disturbing presentiment. More likely, however, Lincoln, despite the repeated warnings from his own subconscious mind, could not consciously accept the message of his imminent demise. It is a terrible thing to look death square in the face and realize it has come for you. In his dreams, Lincoln had attended his own funeral, yet it could not be *he* who lay on the bier at that wake...it was some "other" president.

Now, on the evening before Good Friday, Lincoln had the "usual dream" of the ship sailing towards that "indefinite shore," which he tells us had foretold every major event of the war. Yet the President could not — or would not — see that the momentous event of which his dream foretold was not Sherman's triumph, but his very own murder.

Of all the portents and presentiments ascribed to Lincoln, these two dreams he had in the fortnight before April 14th remain the clearest evidence that Abraham Lincoln may well indeed have been blessed — or cursed — with genuine paranormal gifts.

Although the various primary accounts of the mid-April cabinet meeting do vary in detail, the basic gist of what Lincoln said at the meeting remains remarkably consistent. The men who heard Lincoln's words, moreover, were no woolly-minded mystics or credulous believers. They were hard-headed, pragmatic politicians — men who dealt with cold facts and stark realities. Whatever their spiritual beliefs, they were not inclined to exaggerate, much less fabricate, such an incident.

It has been pointed out by some cynics that General Grant, in his memoirs, fails to note Lincoln's discussion of this dream. The presumption is that had this discussion actually taken place, Grant would surely have made mention of it.

However, as Gideon Welles noted in his diary three days after the event, none of the participants of the April 14th meeting would have taken note of Lincoln's small talk about his dream had he not been murdered that very night. Although Grant neglected to mention this incident, we know from other sources that both Grant and his wife were very much believers in such presentiments.[162]

Chapter 18

Assassination Omens

Treason has done its worst; nor steel nor poison,
Malice domestic, foreign levy, nothing
Can touch him further."

— William Shakespeare, Macbeth

There is a long-standing tradition against attending public celebrations or entertainment on Good Friday. My great-grandmother came over from Ireland during the Civil War at the age of seven; she was still just a youth when Lincoln died, but to her dying day she swore that Lincoln would never have been killed had he not attended theater on the day Christ died. Doubtless there were many Protestants in those days who would also have shared the devout Irish girl's superstition.

While the taboo against going out the day Christ died was not one of the many superstitions Lincoln observed, still, it was one of a number of ill omens that were observed by others at the time of the assassination. To some, such omens may seem less than overwhelming as evidence of paranormal activity. Taken collectively, however, these signs and omens constituted powerful testimony that something beyond the ken of mortal men was at work in the days and hours leading up to Lincoln's assassination.

As we've seen, Lincoln had two particularly dramatic dreams of prophecy in the period before his death; that the President could not — or would not — interpret these warnings correctly goes without saying. However, as strong as these dreams were, they were but two out of many warnings during this same period. A number of documented cases of precognition cluster around the period of early April and all centered on the person of Abraham Lincoln.

On Wednesday, April 6th, an entourage of administration officials, as well as Mrs. Lincoln, had arrived at City Point to join the President. The cabinet members, important senators, and the First Lady, as well as the Marquis de Chambron, found the President holding court aboard the steamboat *River Queen.*

Soon after arriving aboard the *River Queen,* Mary was talking with Abe about the grand tour of Europe they were planning for once the war was finally concluded. The war had been a constant strain on both of them and on their marriage; it had been compounded by the loss of their beloved Willie as well. Now, it seemed to Mary, with the end of the war in sight, all those morbid thoughts her husband had of not outliving the war would be forgotten. They both needed a well-earned vacation.

As they were conversing about the planned European tour, suddenly Abe blurted out, "You can visit Europe, but I never shall." Probing her husband to explain the odd remark, Abe told her he thought he would not visit the Old Country. Mary knew full well from his past comments what he meant: it was his old presentiment that he would not survive the conflict resurfacing again. Lincoln's dark comments in turn put Mary in a fright; soon she too came to believe his gloomy forecast.[163]

A few days later, on April 9th, Lincoln and his entourage of government officials were headed back to Washington aboard the *River Queen.* Taking a break from the sometime heated discussions about Reconstruction, Lincoln engaged his fellow passengers in conversation about literature. In the course of the discussion, Lincoln began reading a passage from Shakespeare's *Macbeth,*

General Ulysses S. Grant and Julia Dent Grant. The Grants were also believers in the paranormal and both tell of having psychic experiences. Grant and his wife were invited to attend the theater with the Lincolns the night of the President's assassination, but Mrs. Grant had a frightening premonition of doom that day and made her husband turn down the invitation.

reading out loud from the scene where King Duncan of Scotland is assassinated by Macbeth:

> "Duncan is in his grave. After life's
> fitful fever he sleeps well;
> Treason has done its worst;
> nor steel nor poison,
> Malice domestic, foreign levy, nothing
> Can touch him further."

Lincoln paused after reading these lines. To all present, it was painfully obvious that the President was visibly affected by the passage. Lincoln repeated the lines again, commenting on it to the group.

The Marquis de Chambron was present when Lincoln read the lines. Well aware of Lincoln's penchant for mysticism, the Marquis theorized that "a vague presentiment" had come over the President on reading the passage. The incident took on ever greater significance a few days later, when on the 14th, like Duncan, Lincoln's "fitful fever" came to a "strange and mysterious" end.[164]

Lincoln was a great fan of the theater; it was one of the few outlets he had during the Rebellion to relieve him of the constant cares of prosecuting the war. It is not known whether Lincoln was aware of the tradition in the theater of the "Curse of the Scottish Play." Actors in England and America have a long-standing superstition that Macbeth is an ill-omened play and that misfortune follows those who recite it. In truth, Macbeth is one of Shakespeare's bloodier dramas and one that deals both with the supernatural and the cold-blooded murder of a ruler. Whenever it is performed, actors believe bad things follow in its wake.

It was this same French visitor who observed Lincoln go in and out of several shallow states of altered consciousness in the space of one evening while aboard the *River Queen*.[165] We know that one of his two most prophetic dreams came to him during this same period while aboard the steamboat, but the President's dreams and presentiments were not isolated incidents. Unbeknownst to Lincoln, signs and warnings were beginning to cluster together, even though on the surface all seemed calm in Washington.

In fact, on the very day of his assassination, Lincoln's frequent veil of doom and gloom was lifted. Cynics point to this to refute the notion that Lincoln was psychic or that his dreams and other reported phenomena were in any way paranormal and prophetic. However, throughout history, from the Old Testament through Merlin and later seers, it is rare to find one who knew their demise was near. It may be a subconscious defense to maintain sanity that those gifted with prophetic foresight are deliberately hindered from realizing the exact hour of their own demise. Nonetheless, there were signs all about, if one were sufficiently aware to heed their import.

After the cabinet meeting of April 14th, Lincoln resolved to take in a theatrical diversion; with the Capitol in a general state of celebration, Lincoln felt some celebratory entertainment was called for — even if the more devout felt it scandalous.

General Grant and his wife were initially invited to attend the show that night at Ford's Theatre with the President and First Lady. After all, who better to share the laurels of victory than with Grant? However, at the last minute, they bowed out, mainly at Julia Grant's insistence. Historians have sometimes attributed this to Julia Grant's dislike of the First Lady. Admittedly, the high-strung Mary was prone to jealous fits — only recently at City Point, she had gone off when she saw her husband riding with another general's wife — but there is no evidence that Julia held any particular grudges against the First Lady. Moreover, we know from Mrs. Grant's own memoirs that this was not the reason. In her memoirs, Julia Dent Grant goes into some detail about that afternoon — and her explanation for turning down the invitation was far from mundane.

The Grants, Julia and Ulysses, were as much believers in destiny, presentiments, and other paranormal phenomena as the Lincolns were — and with equal cause. Just before the War, Grant was to all an abject failure; yet within a few years time he went from nothing to becoming commander of all the armies of the United States and achieved the enduring reputation as one of the great captains of history. If Ulysses S. Grant was not a child of destiny, then surely no one was.

As we've seen during the cabinet meeting, Grant was showcased as the hero of the hour and gave Lincoln's men his account of Lee's surrender. As for Lincoln's account of his prophetic dream, Grant does not appear to have commented on it to his wife later, perhaps because he knew that she, too, was a strong believer in presentiments.

Nonetheless, that afternoon, a feeling of uneasiness began to overtake Julia's mind, as if some unnamed doom was trying to overcome her and her hero husband. When she was informed of their invitation to the theater that night with the Lincolns, she became more agitated. For some cause she could not explain, she was anxious to leave Washington that very afternoon. While her husband was still at the White House, she not only sent a note to the General, but also dispatched three of his staff officers after it to reinforce the message.

"I do not know what possessed me to take such a freak, but go home I felt I must," Julia tells us. Julia also had some odd encounters with strangers that day, including one pretending to be a messenger from Mrs. Lincoln, that also set her on edge. At luncheon with the wife of one of her husband's aides, she said, "I believe there will be an outbreak tonight or soon. I just feel it."[166]

Over at the White House that same afternoon, one of Lincoln's bodyguards, William Crook, also had an odd experience, which, in retrospect, he took for an omen of what was to come.

It was always a habit of Lincoln's before dismissing Crook for the evening to say to his bodyguard "Good night, Crook." It was as regular as clockwork to Crook; the President had never varied this ritual so long as Crook could remember. This evening, however, Lincoln after indicating to Crook that his service would not be needed further, said to his guard, "Goodbye, Crook."

"It startled me...I remember distinctly the shock of surprise and the impression, at the time, that he had never said it before." Crook for a moment thought better of leaving the President after that remark, for the President already had said earlier that day to Crook that he felt he would be assassinated, but by then Lincoln was already gone and Crook had worked past his normal quitting time, so he headed home. The next morning, when Crook heard of the assassination, he remembered the President's fatal farewell the night before.[167]

Elsewhere in the Capitol, other folk were experiencing even weirder omens of something evil afoot. Old "Sis" Thomas, who lived with her children not far from Ford's Theatre, had a reputation as a "conjur woman." Ghosts were always dropping in on Sis Thomas' home for a visit, which never bothered the old woman, for she knew how to talk to them. However, when the dogs kept howling for several days straight and the rooster kept crowing, she began to get spooked.

Finally, "when a large picture of Lincoln fell off the wall and a bird flew into the room," Sis later explained, "I just knew someone was going to die in the neighborhood." The old seeress' uncanny intuition proved all too true.[168]

When the President was finally pronounced dead at 7 a.m. on April 15th, news of his death spread as fast as telegraph and mounted courier could relay the news. However, there was something that relayed the terrible tale even faster: what has sometimes been referred to as the "jungle telegraph."

Far away in the South, troops of Sherman's Army of the Tennessee were still in a state of armed readiness. "Uncle Joe" Johnston's remnants of the once-proud Confederate Army of Tennessee had finally been run to ground in North Carolina and, as with Lee a few days before, everyone knew the end was near. One morning, Major George Putnam, of the 176th New York Volunteer Infantry, was bivouacked with his division in the village of Durham, North Carolina.[169] They had no direct telegraph lines to the outside world, but they generally received dispatches by courier around noon each day. The dispatch rider came through a swamp from a telegraph station that was linked to Wilmington and the North.

That particular April morning, Putnam went over to the shanty of a venerable African American, who served as the local barber, to get a shave. The old man took up his razor, put it down, and then lifted it up again, but was unable to begin his task. The barber's arms were visibly shaking. Finally, he told the major, "Massa, I can't shave yer this mornin'." Putnam could see he was very upset and asked why. "Well, somethin's happened to Massa Linkum," replied the old barber.

The soldier tried to reassure him that they had no news from the government of anything amiss up North. Surely, in this remote post, the army would get word first. The barber, nearly in tears, was insistent, however: "We colored folks — we get news, or we get half news, sooner than you-uns. I don't know jes' what it is, but somethin' has gone wrong with Massa Linkum."

Disturbed, Putnam went over to headquarters to see if any news had arrived that he might not have heard. Other soldiers in the camp, including the division Adjutant, had experienced similar encounters with the local black population and were equally perplexed.

At noon the courier was seen rising across the field. From the man's face, the other soldiers could tell he was bearing bad tidings. His saddle bags carried the regular mail, but he handed a special envelope directly to the Adjutant.

The officer broke open the letter and read the dispatch, but he was unable to read it aloud. A lieutenant took it from his hand, but he, too, was overcome with emotion. All the lieutenant could blurt out was, "Lincoln is dead."[170]

These incidents were by no means the only instances of paranormal activity associated with the murder of Abraham Lincoln. Throughout the land, North and South, to greater or lesser degrees, there were other uncanny indications that something tragic would happen to the nation's leader.

"Father Abraham," some called him. "The Moses of our people," others proclaimed him. All those who had yearned for freedom and fought to preserve the Union mourned his passing. Omens, signs, and presentiments might be deemed coincidence by some or wishful thinking by others, but to those folk who experienced them these preternatural warnings of Lincoln's demise were real indeed.

Chapter 19

A Certain Fatality: The Lincoln "Curse"

"Woe unto the world because of offenses
For it must need be that offenses come;
But woe unto that man by whom the offense cometh!"
                    — *Abraham Lincoln, Second Inaugural Address*

Robert Todd Lincoln, taken during the war. The only one of their four sons to survive into adulthood, Robert Lincoln had a distinguished career in his own right, but he believed that a "certain fatality" occurred when he was too near a U.S. president. He was present when three presidents were assassinated and at other political assassinations.

One still may see from time to time the tabloid press emblazon their front pages with headlines proclaiming "The Curse of the Kennedy's." There is indeed something uncanny about so much woe befalling one famous family. Yet it is far harder to explain the chain of circumstances surrounding the Lincoln Curse.

The Lincoln Curse is not to be confused with "Tecumseh's Curse," which has befallen almost every president elected in a year with zero at the end — including Lincoln — but the Lincoln Curse is specific to Abraham Lincoln and his family.

Even before his untimely but foreseen death, Lincoln and his family had suffered more than their fair share of woe. Eddie, their second-born son, died while still in infancy; Willie died of a fever while in the White House. On Mary's side of the family, a brother and several brothers-in-law all died fighting for the very cause she and her husband opposed. After the war, Mary herself likely, briefly, suffered a nervous breakdown after Tad also died in childhood. Only the eldest son, Robert, lived a long, full life — and he lived to feel the full brunt of the Lincoln Curse.

Robert Lincoln, despite his mother's opposition, volunteered for the Union army and served as a staff officer for General Grant. As it so happened, Robert Lincoln was back in Washington on April 14th, the night his father was assassinated.

Although his army career was brief, Robert Lincoln had been in on the end of the war to witness momentous events and had been with Grant when

Lee surrendered at Appomattox. Robert came home to see his father the morning of the 14th and he, too, had been invited to join his parents at the theater that evening, but he begged off, citing his exhaustion at having just come from the field of battle.

Robert was in his room at the White House when news came of the attack at Ford's Theatre. Robert rushed to Peterson's House to be with his father and stayed with him throughout the night until his father's final moments at seven o'clock the next morning.

Despite a long career of public service, little is publicly known about Robert Todd Lincoln and still less is said. No doubt his private papers could tell much, but they remain moldering away in some dusty archive waiting to see the light of day — assuming he didn't burn those too. Until then, an important piece of the Lincoln puzzle is missing, for not only was he an important figure in his own right, he was also the self-appointed gatekeeper of the Abraham Lincoln legacy.

We know, for example, that at least on one occasion, Robert Lincoln consigned to the flames a large quantity of his father's papers. He did this to keep secret information that he deemed would have cast his martyred father in a less than saintly light. We shall never know precisely what important documents were consigned to the flames, but clearly Robert Lincoln had something to conceal.[171]

In the 1870s, Robert had his mother committed to an insane asylum. Whether this was to "protect her from herself" as he claimed, to get hold of her money as she claimed, or because

her publicly frequenting mediums had become a public embarrassment to him as his committal documents stated, is subject to debate. Most likely Robert was trying to maintain the public image of his father as secular saint; Mary Todd Lincoln's unorthodox behavior regarding séances and Spiritualists certainly was disruptive of his sanitizing effort.

After an insanity "trial," in which her interest in the Spiritualism movement was cited as evidence of her derangement, Mary was locked away at Bellevue Place, an upscale sanitarium for eccentric matrons who had become an embarrassment to their families. For its day, Bellevue Place in Batavia, Illinois, was a relatively enlightened institution and Mary probably did benefit from her brief seclusion there.

However, after a three-month incarceration, Mary had enough. For someone supposedly insane, Mary's campaign to get out of Bellevue demonstrated a great deal of rationality. She smuggled letters out to her lawyer, James Bradwell and his wife Myra, as well as to the editor of the crusading *Chicago Times*. Myra was a close friend of Mary's as well as a pioneering feminist and dedicated Spiritualist. With the adverse publicity proving an embarrassment, Mary was released, but she did not forgive Robert for locking her up.

After burying his father, Robert moved what remained of his family to Chicago, where he completed law school in 1867. After incurring his mother's wrath, Robert may have thought he had enough ill luck. On a public level, at least, Robert Lincoln enjoyed great success.

In 1877, Robert Lincoln was offered the post of Assistant Secretary of State with President Rutherford B. Hayes' administration, but he turned it down. Early in 1881, Robert did accept the post of Secretary of War from President John A. Garfield.

On July 2, 1881, Secretary of War Lincoln was at the Baltimore and Potomac train station in the Capitol to see President Garfield off. Garfield was scheduled to make a speech at Williams College, his alma mater.

Secretary of State James G. Blaine ("that man from Maine") was also present for the send-off. It has been alleged that the President wished to have Lincoln present because he had been having disturbing dreams and, knowing that Robert's father had similar experiences, he wished to discuss them with Robert.

As Garfield entered the waiting room of the terminal, a man stepped behind him and fired point-blank into the President's back. Charles Guiteau was a disgruntled Republican politician — a "Stalwart" — and supposedly murdered the President so that the Vice President would take over. Robert, nearby, heard the two shots ring out. Once again, Robert Lincoln was present at a presidential assassination.

Robert continued to serve under Garfield's successor, but the coincidence of being present at two presidential murders began to weigh on his mind and make him ill-at-ease. In 1885, Robert Todd Lincoln left public service. For several years, he engaged in philanthropy and practiced law.

In 1889, however, Robert was appointed U.S. ambassador to Great Britain under President Benjamin Harrison. Lincoln remained Minister to the Court of St. James until 1893, after which he became general counsel to the Pullman Railroad Car Company, eventually rising to President and then finally Chairman of the Board of the powerful corporation. All during this time, from 1884 to 1912, Robert Todd Lincoln's name came up numerous times as a potential presidential or vice-presidential candidate. However, each time Lincoln denied any interest in high office and actively discouraged any attempts to draft him. Later, Robert explained to Teddy Roosevelt, "I have seen too much of the seamy side of the Presidential robe to think it a desirable garment."

In 1901, as the head of a major transportation company, Robert was invited to the Pan-American Exposition by President William McKinley. On September 6, President McKinley was at the Temple of Music, standing in a receiving line, shaking hands with a long line of citizens. Robert Lincoln had just arrived at the fair, his presidential invitation in hand, when two shots rang out from inside the hall.

A crazed Anarchist, Leon F. Czolgosy, with his gun wrapped up in a bandage in his right hand, had gotten in the receiving line with all the others. When the President went to shake Czolgosy's hand, the assassin fired directly into him twice.

McKinley was rushed to the hospital, where Robert hastened to see him. McKinley died six days later. Again, it has been asserted that McKinley had been bothered by uneasy dreams of foreboding and wished to talk to Robert about these dreams of death. Once again Robert Lincoln had been in the wrong place at the right time.

To be present at one presidential assassination is an unfortunate experience. To be present at the murder of two U.S. presidents is an uncanny coincidence. However, to be witness to three presidential assassinations cannot be dismissed as mere coincidence. Robert Todd Lincoln, common sense lawyer, politician, and businessman, knew that something far greater than random chance was involved in all this.

From 1901 on, Robert Lincoln repeatedly turned down invitations to the White House or any other presidential function. As nominal head of the Republican Party, Lincoln received many such invitations and refused them one and all. Only once, in 1922, did Robert again attend an event when a sitting President was present. It was at the dedication of the Lincoln Memorial in Washington, when President Warren G. Harding and former President Howard Taft were both in attendance. Fortunately, no misfortune befell either chief executive during the gathering.

Robert Todd Lincoln died in 1926, and was buried in Arlington Cemetery in "a nice quiet spot" that he had previously picked out. In 1963, another grave graced Robert's nice quiet spot — the grave of assassinated President John F. Kennedy.

Other uncanny circumstances — some would say synchronicities — seemed to occur about the sixteenth President's son which have added to the aura surrounding the Lincoln Curse. For example, in 1910, Robert Lincoln witnessed an assassination attempt against New York City Mayor Willin Gaynor as well.

There is also the odd fact that Robert Lincoln's life was saved by a member of the Booth family. Actor Edwin Booth did not know who the young man was at the time — it was simply "coincidence" — one of many that seemed to swirl around Robert Lincoln's life.

That an uncanny fate dogged Robert Lincoln may seem clear to us at a distance, but did Robert himself believe in the Lincoln Curse? Although he strove very successfully to suppress evidence of his father's encounters with the paranormal, Robert Todd Lincoln was once heard to say: "There is a certain fatality about presidential functions when I am present."

Robert Lincoln may not have been quite as open as his father had been about his relationship to fate, but he, too, seems to have been a captive of destiny.[172]

Chapter 20

The Afterlife of Our 16th President

"It is portentous, and a thing of state;
That here at midnight in our little town;
A mourning figure walks, and will not rest;
Near the old courthouse pacing up and down."

— Vachel Lindsey, 1931

Lincoln's funeral coach. The Lincoln funeral
train wound its way slowly home to Springfield,
Illinois. The Lincoln ghost train is said to follow
the original route to this very day.

The balcony box seat at Ford's Theatre where Lincoln was assassinated... Lincoln is believed to still haunt the box.

Other than Elvis, perhaps no American figure has had quite so active a post-mortem existence as Abraham Lincoln. While the average ghost chooses a single place to haunt and sticks to it, in death the Great Emancipator has apparently emancipated himself from being bound to just one spot. Old Abe, to judge by numerous reports, evidently has several favorite haunts.

Far and away, the one place most closely tied to Abe's shade is the White House. As a pimply-faced young scholar, I once took the grand tour of the presidential mansion and remember the event well. In truth, however, I cannot recall seeing any lanky gentleman dressed in black and certainly no one wearing a stove-pipe hat. Nonetheless, over the years, quite a few folk who have crossed its threshold did.

The earliest recorded encounter with the dead President in the White House dates back to the Andrew Johnson administration.[173] In 1899, however, one elderly porter who had been on staff since the Lincoln Administration claimed he daily saw and conversed with the spirits of Presidents Lincoln, Grant, and Garfield.[174]

One of the more recent incidents involved White House Chief Usher Gary Walter. One day, during the previous administration, he was standing at the threshold to the stairs leading down to the ground floor, along with three Capitol police. All of a sudden, the three of them felt a sudden gust of cold air rush past, shortly followed by seeing heavy doors close shut with a bang.

Gary Walter swore that the doors were too substantial to just swing shut on their own; they always have to be shut manually. Gary and the police went over to the doors to see if something natural had caused the doors to shut themselves — there wasn't. He and his associates believed the cause was not natural but supernatural.[175]

Others who have either stayed or worked in the White House have had similar uncanny experiences. Although there have been the occasional weird encounter on the ground level, most reported paranormal experiences seem to occur on the second floor — the area reserved for the First Family and guests of state.

For example, during the 1960s, Lady Bird Johnson, President Lyndon Johnson's wife, reported feeling an uncanny chill while watching television one evening in her personal quarters — she was watching a documentary about Abraham Lincoln at the time. On another occasion, Lynda Bird, President Johnson's daughter, reported having someone knock on her door one evening. When she opened it, no one was visible.

President Teddy Roosevelt is reported to have sighted Lincoln in several rooms of the White House. According to one National Park Service executive, Lincoln's spirit has been seen walking up and down the second floor hallway, knocking on doors. Grace Coolidge, Calvin Coolidge's significant other, allegedly saw a figure clad in black, with a shawl draped over his shoulders — as Lincoln was known to do to

keep out the chill of the Washington winter night air.

During World War II, Queen Wilhelmina, sovereign of the Netherlands, stayed at the White House as a guest. She was staying in the Rose Room (now the Queen's Bedroom Suite) when one night there was a knock on the door. She opened the door and there before her loomed Honest Abe, large as death. The Queen fainted straightaway; when she awoke on the floor, the apparition was gone.

To judge from the accumulated reports of White House ghost sightings, far and away the most haunted spot in the entire building is the Lincoln Bedroom.

Sir Winston Churchill was another wartime guest of the FDR White House. From December 22, 1941, to January 3, 1943, the British Prime Minister stayed with Roosevelt and was billeted in the Lincoln Bedroom. One night, not long after settling into the Lincoln Bedroom suite, Churchill was taking a bath after a long day of discussions with FDR and his advisors. The United States had just entered the war and the Prime Minister had come in person to make sure he and the President were on the same page in prosecuting the war. Apparently, Churchill was fond of relaxing in the bath with a cigar in one hand and a glass of scotch in the other.

Getting out of the bath, the Prime Minister went into the main part of the bedroom, only to find himself staring face-to-face with Lincoln's apparition. With typical British sang froid, Churchill is alleged to have said,

"You have the better of me, Sir." Still naked, with scotch in hand, Churchill stood there as he watched Lincoln's shade slowly fade to nothing.

Churchill was so disturbed by the confrontation, however, that he refused to remain in the Lincoln Bedroom for the rest of his stay and moved to a bedroom across the hall. Churchill needn't have feared, however — Lincoln was a teetotaler.[176]

Eleanor Roosevelt never personally saw Lincoln in the room, but she swore she could feel his presence there. Her personal secretary, however, passed by the bedroom once and claimed to see the sixteenth President sitting in there putting on a pair of boots. FDR's valet also came upon Lincoln unexpectedly once and ran screaming from the White House shouting he had seen Lincoln's ghost.

Over the years the Lincoln Bedroom has acquired such a reputation that some White House staff refuse to even enter the room. Not so for Amy Carter and her girlfriends. They got hold of a ouija board and tried to get in touch with the Great Emancipator. They were not successful, but apparently Maureen Reagan and her husband were unwilling hosts to Lincoln's ghost in there one night.[177]

Although the Lincoln Bedroom definitely seems to be Father Abraham's favorite abode, the room actually was never Lincoln's bedroom. Before 1902, the bedroom suite actually served as the presidential offices and cabinet meeting room. This was the room in which the Emancipation Proclamation was signed. It was also the same room in which Lincoln had his last cabinet meeting on April 14, 1865; four chairs from that meeting still abide in the room along with the President's ghost.

While Abraham Lincoln is the most frequently seen specter in the White House, he is no means alone. Other members of the Lincoln family, not to mention other presidents and their kith and kin, have been seen in and around the White House over the years. An antique Redcoat holding a flaming torch has even made the occasional appearance.

Though Lincoln's appearance is not a common occurrence, he has been seen enough by witnesses over the years to give credence to the belief in his ghost. It has also been pointed out that Abe is most frequently seen during times of national crisis.[178]

Our sixteenth president has been sighted elsewhere as well. Perhaps the strangest of such Lincoln ghost sightings are the sightings of the Lincoln Ghost Train.

After the assassination, Lincoln's mortal remains were embalmed and prepared for burial, but his body was not interred in Washington, D.C., or anywhere else right away. His body lay in state at the Capitol Rotunda and then a unique train was assembled to transport him to his home in Springfield, Illinois, traveling through a number of northern cities and states along the way.

This long pilgrimage home by rail in 1865 was Abraham Lincoln's final farewell to the nation and his last physical journey, but it was by no means Lincoln's last rail sojourn.[179]

No one is quite sure when people first started reporting seeing the Lincoln Ghost Train. I remember hearing about it as a boy from my father; his dad had been a railroad engineer who ran trains around upstate New York and he may well have been the one who relayed the story to my father. Certainly a number of early reports emanate from upstate New York, but there have also been accounts of the Ghost Train from places all along the route of the original funeral train.

For many decades now, between April 21st and May 2nd of every year, they say the phantom train wends its way home to Springfield. Through small towns and big cities, through countryside where tracks no longer lay, a weird procession of otherworldly demeanor makes its eerie way.

Just like the original, an antique engine pulls old wooden passenger cars, followed by the large Lincoln funeral coach, with assorted other rolling stock bringing up the rear. In the reported incidents, though, only the Ghost Train emanates an eerie bluish caste. Up the Hudson Valley and through western New York, it silently glides in the night, through Ohio, Indiana, and finally Illinois, as it chugs towards Lincoln's hometown.

Some claim a crew of skeletons man the train, clad in ragged uniforms of army blue. In some cases, people have reported seeing it in a cornfield where no tracks can be found. The railroad ceased to run that way many years ago…and yet the Ghost Train noiselessly glides across this field as if it were still 1865.

In Urbana, no one has actually seen the Ghost Train, but every April, about the same time each year, railroad crossing gates seem to malfunction with uncanny regularity. Near the right-of-way, residents say they hear phantom whistles and see smoke plumes where no locomotive can be seen. A few years back, one earnest ghost-hunting group in Ohio camped out in a pasture. All the ghost hunters got were some chiggers and perhaps a slight chill.[180]

Other Lincoln hauntings have been reported at Fort Monroe, Virginia, where Lincoln occasionally stayed in a billet called "Old Quarters Number One." His shade is occasionally also spotted at Ford's Theatre, the scene of his murder.

Lincoln has even made his presence known in Loudonville, New York, where Clara Harris lived; Harris was the young lady in the theater box when the President was assassinated on April 14th — her dress was splattered with Lincoln's blood and brain matter that night.

When her home in New York began experiencing strange phenomena, Clara blamed the dress and went to the extent of walling up the closet in which it hung. All this was to no avail — the invisible shade continued to disturb the house with poltergeist activity.[181]

Mary Lincoln and one of her sons haunt a village in Vermont. Originally intended to be the Lincolns' vacation spot in the summer of '65, Mrs. Lincoln and Tad later stayed at the Equinox in Manchester Center, Vermont. The scenic mountain village was perhaps one of Mary's few happy memories after her husband's death; it is perhaps on this account she dwells there still.[182]

It has been a tradition of long-standing in Springfield, Illinois, that the city's most famous scion haunts his hometown. As Vachel Lindsey indicated in his famous poem about Lincoln's ghost, the mourning figure in "suit of ancient black" has been reported at several locations around town.

Given Lincoln's ghostly presence in other places, it comes as little surprise that his Springfield home has also been claimed as haunted by the Prairie Lawyer. Although the National Parks Service officially denies that Lincoln's home is haunted, visitors and a few former workers there say otherwise.

One former Lincoln home staffer was interviewed by the *Springfield State Journal-Register* some years back. While she never actually saw the figure of Lincoln in the house, she reported numerous uncanny experiences while working there. Lincoln's favorite rocking chair, for example, would start rocking all on its own. Various artifacts of the Lincoln family would also be found to have moved from room to room (a curatorial no-no), while some pieces of the house museum's collection would disappear entirely, only to reappear days later. All of this was most curious.[183]

Oak Ridge Cemetery, Lincoln's final resting place, has also had a reputation for being haunted. When the Lincoln funeral train finally arrived into Springfield in May 1865, the martyred president did not rest in peace. A grand tomb was planned and he had to be housed in temporary quarters, but even after he was given a proper tomb, a group of ghoulish grave-robbers tried to steal his body.

After that, a more secure sepulcher was begun and once more his mortal remains' final rest was postponed. During this prolonged burial and reburial, the first reports of the cemetery's hauntings began to surface. Since then the sound of invisible footsteps, disembodied voices, and the occasional sighting of a spectral Lincoln, have all been reported at one time or another.[184]

In the heart of the historic part of town, near the old county courthouse where Lincoln once practiced law, as well as the nearby market, Honest Abe has also been alleged to make the rounds. As the Vachel Lindsey poem chronicles, his tall black-clad figure has been reported to wander there late at night "until a spirit-dawn shall come."

The poem, based as it was on the local legend, was inspired by a race riot that had broken out in Springfield the year before. In 1931, Vachel Lindsey was shocked that in Lincoln's own hometown racism was still present while abroad the evil of Fascism was growing stronger everyday; Lindsey imagined what the Great Emancipator's shade might say to these tyrannies.

To Lindsey, the reason Lincoln's restless shade still walks among us is because, "the sins of all the war-lords burn his heart." Lincoln cannot rest, the Troubadour Poet informs us, until peace and liberty are brought once more to "cornland, Alp and Sea."

If that truly is the cause of Lincoln's shade's restlessness, then doubtless he walks among us still.

Chapter 21

Conclusion

"Every known fact in natural science was divined by the presentiment of somebody,
before it was actually verified."

— Ralph Waldo Emerson

I n chronicling Lincoln's relationship with the paranormal, we have largely adhered to the documentary record and tried to avoid unnecessary speculation. Doubtless buried unpublished in some archive or hidden in an old newspaper account are incidents that we have overlooked, but what has been found points clearly to Lincoln's firm belief in an array of paranormal phenomena.

Previous historians have at times written about one or another of these paranormal incidents; usually by the more popular writers such as Carl Sandburg or Jim Bishop, where their goal was mainly to liven up a long narrative with interesting or unusual anecdotes. Few historians have taken these incidents seriously or looked at them as a whole. Within these few pages we have sought to rectify this oversight and thereby provide fresh insight into Abraham Lincoln the man, his career and the times he lived in.

Nonetheless, Lincoln often presents a study in contradictions. His close friend Ward Hill Lamen asserts that he was no "dabbler in divination"; yet we know Lincoln frequented a voodoo fortune-teller, closely observed signs and omens, and had numerous prophetic dreams, which clearly weighed heavily on his mind.

In his young manhood, Lincoln's attitude towards religion seems to have bordered on atheism. While his early skepticism gave way to faith, throughout his life Lincoln put great store in mathematics and science. This facet of Lincoln's personality also seems greatly at variance with his self-admitted "superstitious nature" and his life-long belief in a personal destiny.

Lincoln's rational nature often seemed at odds with his many uncanny beliefs. How did Lincoln himself square such things as presentiments and prophetic dreams with reason and nature?

If we go by what Lincoln told his friend Ward Hill Lamon, Lincoln did not regard the paranormal phenomena that he so closely observed as being within the realm of the supernatural at all. Instead, to Lincoln, such things as premonitions and similar phenomena proceeded from the natural order of things. He felt the phenomena were not supernatural but *preternatural.*

The motive power behind all such phenomena Lincoln ascribed to the "Almighty intelligence that governs the universe," these processes conforming to natural laws. "Nature," said Lincoln, "is the workmanship of the Almighty; and we form links in the general chain of intellectual and material life."[185]

Lincoln's metaphysical beliefs closely correspond to his more familiar political philosophy. It is well known that Lincoln trusted in the political wisdom of "the common people." Lincoln once commented that he esteemed the "collective wisdom" of the common folk above "the highest gifts of cultured men." Since prophetic dreams and presentiments were natural occurrences (in Lincoln's view), the best interpreters of such phenomena were the "common people," whom he often referred to as "the children of nature."

Lincoln's faith in the wisdom of the common man therefore extended into the para-psychological realm as well as the political. Whatever obtained general credence among these "children of nature," must have some basis in truth, Lincoln believed. Of course, having passed the greater part of his life among "the common people," Lincoln regarded himself as one of their number.[186]

Needless to say, Lincoln's interpretation of paranormal phenomena is not the only spin that has been put on his many weird encounters and altered states. John T. Stuart, a former law partner of Lincoln's, theorized that Lincoln's abnormal dreams and strange visions were all the fault of digestive abnormalities. Lincoln's liver, Stuart informs us, "failed to work properly — did not secrete bile — and his bowels were equally as inactive."[187]

If Stuart's cynical explanation of Lincoln's uncanny experiences sound a bit Dickensian in tone, the connection may be more than coincidental. The character Ebenezer Scrooge in Dickens' *A Christmas Carol* likewise ascribed his supernatural visions to poor digestion. We know that the story of Lincoln's prophetic dream "of a ship sailing rapidly" was a favorite anecdote of Charles Dickens, who told and retold it — with embellishments — to all and sundry.[188] Aware as he was of Lincoln's predilection for paranormal phenomena, one may posit that the great author may also have incorporated Stuart's cynical explanation for it into his classic tale of the supernatural.

While the society and culture in which Lincoln grew up strongly affected his belief system, it does not readily explain Lincoln's own personal experiences of uncanny phenomena. His well-documented altered states of consciousness, his visions, his firmly rooted belief in a foreordained personal destiny and high mission...all these cannot simply be ascribed to cultural conditioning — or bad digestion.

If there is one incident that we can pinpoint, which may have served as the trigger that unleashed Lincoln's uncanny personal experiences, it is his Near Death Experience (or NDE) in early life. The fact that Lincoln nearly died and seemingly came back from the dead is an incontestable fact; what consequences flowed from that event has been the subject of widely varying interpretation.

It is, in fact, only in recent decades that the phenomenon of NDE has been studied systematically by doctors and psychologists, with a high proportion of individuals who have gone through such events and subsequently had paranormal experiences (more than 25%) being documented in the clinical literature on the subject. While we may not be able to prove beyond a doubt that this was indeed the cause of Lincoln's occult experiences, it is a factor at least worthy of serious consideration. Moreover, many survivors of NDE come back to life with a sense of renewed mission in life; at least on a psychological level this certainly seems true of Lincoln as well.

The fact that Lincoln put such great stock in signs and omens could be explained by his cultural environment — certainly he was not alone in such beliefs. However, in other areas, Lincoln rejected many aspects of that same culture, such as his family's "hard shell" Calvinism that said most people were predestined to

Hell no matter what kind of life they lived. Lincoln did believe in destiny... just not of that sort.

In an interview with Herndon, William Hannah asserted that Lincoln was "a kind of universalist — that he never could bring himself to the belief in Eternal punishment."[189] In his rejection of eternal damnation, Lincoln shared much in common with spiritualist belief.

Perhaps the most disputed aspect of Lincoln's relationship to paranormal belief and practice was his involvement with Spiritualism. The traditional viewpoint of historians has only reluctantly, if at all, conceded any connection between Lincoln and séances. This, we have seen, is clearly wrong.

During his presidency, Abraham Lincoln was equally interested in attending séances as his wife Mary, nor were his motivations for so doing simply to humor her. Quite the contrary, there is substantive evidence to indicate that Abe's engagement with mediums was as great as his wife's and that his interest in Spiritualist ideas may well date back to his Springfield days. This is not to say, however, that either Abraham or Mary considered themselves Spiritualists, as some adherents of the movement have claimed. Despite her continued frequenting of mediums in the years after her husband's death, in 1872 Mary adamantly proclaimed that "I am not either a Spiritualist!" Likewise, with Abraham, just as he was "not a technical Christian" one may also infer that he was also not a "technical" spiritualist.

Clearly, however, Abraham Lincoln was fascinated by the subject and sought out a number of different mediums while in the White House. Lincoln, though, never openly proclaimed himself a believer while a number of other Republican politicians did.

One thing we may be sure of: Lincoln never blindly followed the advice he received from the "spirits" uncritically. Even some leading Spiritualists of his era concede as much. In any case, where we have detailed accounts of their spirit guides' advice to Lincoln, it was largely hortatory in nature and generally in line with the President's own convictions; that the President had the spirit world on his side would have been comforting, but even if that weren't the case, Lincoln would likely have gone and done what he thought right anyway.

Whether any of the mediums whose séances Lincoln attended were actually in contact with the dead is impossible to prove one way or another. Moreover, such assertions are outside the limits of our historical study. However, some of the physical phenomena exhibited at these sessions, especially the ones hosted by the Lauries and their circle, hint less of contact with the other side, so much as with the inside.

In the early 1970s, researchers with the Toronto Society for Psychical Research conducted a series of experiments to test the hypothesis that some of the ghostly phenomena reported in the more legitimate nineteenth century séances may not have been caused by the spirits of the dead so much as the minds of the living.

The Toronto researchers conducted "sittings" in which they consciously fabricated a fictitious spirit they called "Philip," for whom they created a complete biography. At first they simply sat in a fully lit room and tried to meditate on the agreed upon subject and to visualize it, all to no avail.

However, when the researchers changed methods and reverted to the classic nineteenth century methods, sitting around a table with the lights dimmed, singing psalms, and the like, they began to get results. Although well aware that Philip was their own creation, the psychic researchers began to get rapping sounds, which soon began to respond to yes or no questions. From there, Philip began to make knocking sounds all around the room, moving furniture and dimming the lights up and down. In some cases, the psychokinetic activity was quite dramatic.

The Philip séances demonstrated that phenomena, which sincere Spiritualists may have thought were messages from the dead, may well have been products of the collective unconscious of the spiritualist circle itself. Some nineteenth century spiritualists may have possibly tapped into some kind of genuine paranormal phenomena — just not quite the sort they thought they had.[190]

In a radio interview several years back, Mitch Horowitz, another chronicler of the esoteric aspects of American history and culture, was discussing Abraham Lincoln and Spiritualism. Horowitz, who acknowledged that while some mediums may be genuine, expressed the belief that about 95% of all modern mediums "probably can't do what they say." His comments are reminiscent of what a researcher in another controversial field, Dr. Alan J. Hynek, once made.

Dr. Hynek was a respected scientist and a dedicated debunker of UFOs. For years he went around the country lecturing on the subject, making the claim that 95% of all UFO sightings could be explained away by natural causes, but then one day Dr. Hynek had an epiphany of sorts: he realized that it didn't matter whether 95% of all such incidents could be explained away — it was that unexplainable 5% that mattered! The facts hadn't changed, just his perspective on them. Dr. Hynek went from a denier of UFO phenomena to a believer.

In the Newtonian world of eighteenth century and early nineteenth century science, everything was perfectly explainable by a set of fixed mathematical formulae; not surprisingly, the notion that God was some passive "clock-maker" was very popular among intellectuals of the day. In such a world view, paranormal phenomena were simply the "delusions of the masses."

However, in a Quantum universe, where paradox has become a commonplace fact of science, many phenomena thought impossible now become at least worthy of investigation. Many aspects of the paranormal previously rejected out of hand are increasingly being taken seriously by research scientists. In recent years, experimental physicists have begun to conduct experiments to test whether human consciousness can in fact affect the material world; in some cases, the experiments seem to have proven successful. The laws of science are not a fixed boundary anymore; they are merely the limits of an ever expanding frontier.

That being said, we should also bear in mind that science does not have a monopoly on truth. Preternatural phenomena, which are essentially qualitative in nature, are notoriously hard to subject to the quantitative methods of science. An individual may have a genuine psychic experience but once in a lifetime and never again. Paranormal phenomena may be quite real to those who experience them, but not necessarily to those who don't.

Lincoln experienced many things which could all be put under the general rubric of paranormal, that much is certain. They were part and parcel of his belief system, as well as that of many of those who were around him. Lincoln was by no means abnormal in this regard. Many folk, high and low, held to similar beliefs. Can we prove today that what Lincoln experienced was genuine paranormal phenomena? No more than we can prove they were not.

In the preceding pages, we have put together an array of information based on primary sources that clearly demonstrate Abraham Lincoln's belief in, and observations of, paranormal phenomena. Chronicling these aspects of Abraham Lincoln — and of his paranormal presidency — does not in any way diminish his achievements. It does, however, give us some insight into the wellsprings of his achievements.

Abraham Lincoln preserved the Union from a mortal threat, he moved forward the causes of liberty and justice, and he laid the foundations for a modern industrial nation that has become the light of the world. He believed he was destined to lead the nation in its hour of crisis and decision. Could a man not so gifted with a preternatural belief in his own mission been able to accomplish so much?

Lincoln was not just a great political leader; he was a man of vision. All we have become in the last century and a half and all that we shall be in the centuries to come were begun in the brief span of years during Lincoln's presidency. Lincoln firmly believed in his destiny and that he had a mission to fulfill. His reason and his intellect were tools that helped him achieve that mission, but so too were his preternatural intuition and his implicit faith in his ultimate destiny. In the end, Lincoln fulfilled that destiny — and we are all the better for it.

Appendix

❋ Literature of the Paranormal Presidency

While the following are by no means proof of Lincoln's paranormal experiences, they do demonstrate a popular awareness of Lincoln's encounters with the uncanny. Nonetheless, they are intended more for your edification than as documentary proof.

❋ O Captain! My Captain!
Walt Whitman (1865)

Lincoln's fateful dream of "some singular indescribable vessel" moving towards an indefinite shore became public knowledge within a short time after his assassination and was the inspiration behind one of Walt Whitman's most famous poems. It first appeared in print in *The Saturday Press*, on November 4, 1865; it was later included in Whitman's famous collection of poems, *Leaves of Grass*.

O Captain! My Captain! Our fearful trip is done,
The ship has weather'd every rack, the prize we sought is won,
The port is near, the bells I hear, the people all exulting.
While follow eyes the steady keel, the vessel grim and daring;
But O heart! heart! heart!
O the bleeding drops of red,
Where on the deck my Captain lies,
Fallen cold and dead.

O Captain! My Captain! Rise up and hear the bells;
Rise up—for you the flag is flung—for you the bugle trills,
For you bouquets and ribbon'd wreaths—for you the shores a-crowding,

For you they call, the swaying mass, their eager faces turning;
Here Captain! dear father!
This arm beneath your head!
It is some dream that on the deck,
You've fallen cold and dead.

My Captain does not answer, his lips are pale and still,
My father does not feel my arm, he has no pulse nor will,
The ship is anchor'd safe and sound, its voyage closed and done,
From fearful trip the victor ship comes in with object won;
Exult O shores, and ring O bells!
But I with mournful tread,
Walk the deck my Captain lies,
Fallen cold and dead.

✳ Abraham Lincoln Walks at Midnight

Vachel Lindsay (1879-1931)

The tradition that Lincoln's ghost haunts Springfield, Illinois, is of long-standing. Vachel Lindsay was also a native of the city. When a race riot broke out in his and Lincoln's hometown, he was inspired to write this poem, which also expresses concern about the growing threat of World War.

In Springfield, Illinois

It is portentous, and a thing of state
That here at midnight, in our little town
A mourning figure walks, and will not rest,
Near the old court-house, pacing up and down.

Or by his homestead, or by shadowed yards
He lingers where his children used to play,
Or through the market, on the well-worn stones
He stalks until the dawn-stars burn away.

A bronzed, lank man! His suit of ancient black,
A famous high top-hat, and plain worn shawl
Make him the quaint, great figure that men love,
The prairie-lawyer, master of us all.

He cannot sleep upon his hillside now.
He is among us:–as in times before!
And we who toss or lie awake for long
Breathe deep, and start, to see him pass the door.

His head is bowed. He thinks on men and kings.
Yea, when the sick world cries, how can he sleep?
Too many peasants fight, they know not why,
Too many homesteads in black terror weep.

The sins of all the war-lords burn his heart.
He sees the dreadnaughts scouring every main.
He carries on his shawl-wrapped shoulders now
The bitterness, the folly and the pain.

He cannot rest until a spirit-dawn
Shall come–the shining hope of Europe free:
The league of sober folk, the Workers' Earth,
Bringing long peace to Cornland, Alp and Sea.

It breaks his heart that kings must murder still,
That all his hours of travail here for men
Seem yet in vain. And who will bring white peace
That he may sleep upon his hill again?

Introduction

1 Lloyd Lewis, *Myths After Lincoln*, (Gloucester Mass: P. Smith, 1973; first pub. 1929), 334.
2 Ward Hill Lamon, *Recollections of Abraham Lincoln*. (Washington, DC: by the editor, 1911), 111.

Chapter 1

3 For the differing cultural inheritance between New England and the Southern frontier, see *Albion's Seed: Four British Folkways in America*. (NY: Oxford University Press, 1989).
4 William H. Herndon and Jessie W. Weik, *Life of Lincoln*, (Cleveland: World Publishing, 1949) (hereafter cited as *Life*), 55; on Southern witchcraft also see Christopher K. Coleman, *Strange Tales of the Dark and Bloody Ground*, (Nashville: Rutledge Hill Press, 1998), 37-44; Christopher K. Coleman, *Ghosts and Haunts of Tennessee*, (Winston-Salem, NC: John F. Blair, 2011), 48-56, 128-132.
5 Herndon, *Life*, 56.
6 Herndon, *Life*, 71-72.
7 "Joseph Gillespie to William Herndon," January 31, 1866, Douglas L. Wilson and Rodney Davis, *Herndon's Informants* (hereafter as HI). (Champaign, IL: University of Illinois Press, 1997), 168; Frances Todd Wallace Interview, ibid, #384, 485.
8 Herndon, *Life*, 56.
9 Charlotte Bronte, *Jane Eyre*, (NY: Penguin, 1966) (originally published, London: 1847), 249.
10 J. M. Buckley, "Presentiments, Visions, and Apparitions," *Century Magazine*, Vol. 38, No. 3 (July 1889), 453.
11 Buckley, ibid, 453
12 General John Gordon, CSA, *Reminiscences of the Civil War*, (NY: Scribners, 1903), 65.
13 Julia Dent Grant, *The Personal Memoirs of Julia Dent Grant*, (NY: Putnams, 1975), 92-93.
14 Gordon, ibid.

Chapter 2

15 Ward Hill Lamon, *Recollections of Abraham Lincoln*. (Washington D.C.: the editor, 1911), 110.
16 Lamon, ibid, 111.
17 William H. Herndon and Jessie W. Weik, *Herndon's Lincoln, the True Story of a Great Life* (hereafter cited as *Herndon's Lincoln*).(Springfield, IL: Herndon's Lincoln Publ. Co., 1921), Volume III, 436.
18 Lamon, *Recollections*, 111.

19 Herndon, *Herndon's Lincoln*, Volume I, 51.
20 See, Edward J. Kempf, MD, "Abraham Lincoln's Organic and Emotional Neurosis," *AMA Archives of Neurology and Psychiatry*, Vol. 67, No. 4 (April, 1952), 419-433. (accessed online, December 21, 2000, at www.lincolnportrait.com/ama.html); also Gabor S. Boritt and Adam Boritt, "Lincoln and Marfan Syndrome, the Medical Diagnosis of a Historical Figure," *Civil War History*, Vol. 29, No. 3 (September, 1983), 213-29; Webb Garrison, *The Lincoln No One Knows*. (Nashville: Rutledge Hill Press, 1993), 14-18.
21 Hertz, *The Hidden Lincoln*, (NY: Blue Ribbon Books, 1940); Herndon to J. Weik (Feb. 1, 1891), 262-263.
22 Marquis de Chambron, "Personal Recollections of Mr. Lincoln," *Scribner's Magazine*, Vol.43, No. 1 (January, 1893), 26, 32.
23 David Sunfellow, "Parting Visions," NHNE website, January 6, 1995 (after Dr. Barry Melvin Morse's research); Dannion Brinkley, *Saved by the Light* (NY, 1994).
24 Lamon, *Recollections*, 111.

Chapter 3

25 Herndon, *Herndon's Lincoln*, Vol. I, 62-63.
26 Douglas L. Wilson, "Keeping Lincoln's Secrets." *Atlantic Monthly*, May, 2000: 78-88.
27 Richard Campanella, *Lincoln in New Orleans, the 1828-1831 Faltboat Voyages and their Place in History*, (Lafayette, LA: UL Lafayette Press, 2010), 54
28 Herndon, *Herndon's Lincoln*, Vol. I, 72-73.
29 Isaac N. Arnold, *The Life of Abraham Lincoln*, (Chicago: Jansen McClung, 1885), Vol. I, 31; Alexander J. K. McClure, *"Abe" Lincoln's Yarns and Stories*, (Philadelphia, PA: John C. Winston, 1904), part 4.
30 Arnold, 31.
31 Carl Sandburg, *Abraham Lincoln, the Prairie Years and the War Years*, (NY: Houghton Mifflin Harcourt, 2002), 496.

Chapter 4

32 See, for example, Julia Taft Bayne's comments in this vein, *Tad Lincoln's Father*, (Boston, Little Brown, 1931), 15-16.
33 Herndon, *Life*, 155-167.
34 Ibid, 166.
35 Elizabeth Todd Edwards interview, *Herndon's Lincoln*, No. 332: 443.
36 Ibid.
37 Ibid.
38 Ward Hill Lamon, *Recollections*, 21.
39 Herndon, *Herndon's Lincoln*, 237-38.
40 Lamon, *Recollections*, 21.

41 (Mrs. Lincoln to Herndon), Herndon, *Herndon's Lincoln*, 433.

Chapter 5

42 *New York Daily Tribune*, 7 and 8 November, 1860: 8.

43 Noah Brooks, "Personal Recollections of Abraham Lincoln," *Harper's New Monthly Magazine*, July 1865, 225.

44 Ibid 225.

45 Both Ward Hill Lamon and Richard Carpenter say Lincoln told them of the incident in June 1864, during his re-nomination. Brooks says Lincoln told him shortly after his re-election in November 1864. See Richard Carpenter, *Six Months in the White House*, 163-65; Lamon, *Recollections*, 112-113; Brooks, ibid, 224-225.

46 Brooks, ibid, 225.

47 Carpenter, *Six Months*, 164.

48 See Joe Nickell, "Paranormal Lincoln," *Skeptical Inquirer*, May/June 1999; accessed online March 29, 2011 via the CISCOP website (Committee for the Scientific Investigation of Claims of the Paranormal).

49 Ward Hill Lamon, *Recollections*, 112.

Chapter 6

50 Webb Garrison, *The Lincoln No One Knows*, (Nashville: Rutledge Hill Press, 1999), 250. Also see John Eaton and Ethel Osgood Mason, *Grant, Lincoln and the Freedmen: Reminiscences of the Civil War*, (NY: Longmans, 1907), 89. Lincoln initially viewed it as a sign; he later rephrased it for the devout chaplain to seem more as a symbolic intent.

51 First Inaugural Address, March 4, 1861, in Roy P. Basler, (Ed). *Collected Works of Abraham Lincoln, 1809-1865*. (Princeton, 1953), Vol. IV, 262-271. (Hereafter cited as Basler, *Collected Works*.)

52 Noah Brooks, "Personal Recollections of Abraham Lincoln," *Harper's New Monthly Magazine*, July 1865.

53 Ibid

54 S. P. Chase to Mary Todd Lincoln, 4 March 1865, Abraham Lincoln Papers, Series 1, General Correspondence, 1833-1916, Library of Congress.

55 *London Spectator*, March 5, 1865.

56 "Second Inaugural Address," (March 4, 1865), in Basler, *Collected Works*, VII, 332-333.

Chapter 7

57 Carl Schurz, *The Reminiscences of Carl Schurz*, (NY: Methuen, 1907-08), Vol. II, 225-228.

58 See, for example, Noah Brooks, *Washington in Lincoln's Time* (NY: Century, 1895), 176; Marquis de Chambron, "Personal Recollections," 37.

Chapter 8

59 For more details about the symbolism of the American flag and the war, see the Smithsonian website article, "The Star Spangled Banner: the Flag in the Civil War." (http://americanhistory.si.edu/starspangledbanner/the-flag-in-the-civil-war.aspx)

60 Julia Taft Bayne, *Tad Lincoln's Father*, 114-117.

61 Michael Spangler, "Benjamin Brown French in the Lincoln Period," *White House History*, No. 8, 4-5.

62 N. P. Willis, in Julia Taft Bayne, 117-118.

63 *Diary of Horatio Nelson Taft, 1861-1865*, Vol. I, June 29, 1861; Library of Congress, accessed via American Memory.

64 Julia Taft Bayne, ibid, 117.

Chapter 9

65 George P. Rawick, (Ed.), *The American Slave, a Composite Autobiography*. Westport, CT: Greenwood Press, 2000; via "Civilians in Wartime," blog (at wordpress.com).

66 For the historical background to comets as ill omens in general, see Christopher Kiernan Coleman, "Of Comets, Kings and Dragons."

67 For the scientific details of the comet, see cosmetography.com, "C/1861 J1" (Great Comet of 1861).

68 Cf. James R. Aswell (Ed.) *God Bless the Devil* (Knoxville: UT Press, 1985), 126-127; for more on Granny Weiss (a.k.a. "Mammy Wise"), see Christopher Kiernan Coleman, *Ghosts and Haunts of Tennessee* (Winston-Salem, NC: John F. Blair, 2011).

69 Library of Congress, Graphic Arts Files PR-022-3-29-45, PR-022-3-32-50. (Originals in the New York Historical Society collections)

70 Donald W. Olson and Laurie E. Jasinaki, "Lincoln's Celestial Comet," *Sky and Telescope*, Vol. 117, No. 3 (March 2009), 66ff.

71 Steven Finacom, "Lincoln, a Comet and the Politics of a Nation Divided," *The Berkeley Daily Planet*, October 2, 2009. The preacher's description of the 1858 comet as a "besom of destruction" is eerily similar to the ancient Chinese concept of the comet as "broom star."

72 Julia Taft Bayne, *Tad Lincoln's Father*, ibid, 77-78.

73 "Mrs. Luther Fowler (George Washington) to Abraham Lincoln," March 19,1865, Library of Congress, Abraham Lincoln

Papers, Series 1. General Correspondence. 1833-1916.

Chapter 10

74 For the evolution of Lincoln's and the public's attitudes towards emancipation, see James M. McPherson, *Battle Cry of Freedom* (NY: Oxford, 1988), 490-505.

75 Albert E. Pillsbury, *Lincoln and Slavery* (Boston & NY: Houghton Mifflin, 1913), 80; Basler, *Collected Works*, Volume 7, 282.

76 Joseph Gillespie to Herndon, December 8, 1866, Hertz, *The Hidden Lincoln*, 322-323.

77 Gideon Wells, *The Diary of Gideon Welles* (NY: Houghton Mifflin, 1911), Volume I, 143.

78 Ibid.

Chapter 11

79 See, for example, J. G. Randall, *Lincoln the President*, (NY, 1945) who dismisses it as "melancholy"; or Stephen B. Oates, *With Malice Towards None*, (NY, 1977), who views it as a symptom of clinical depression.

80 Joseph Gillespie to William Herndon, Dec. 8, 1866; in Wilson and Davis, *HI*, 506.

81 Herndon, *Life of Lincoln*.

82 Herndon, *Life of Lincoln*, Vol. III, 436.

83 Emanuel Hertz, *The Hidden Lincoln*, 322.

84 See Allen C. Guelzo, "Abraham Lincoln and the Doctine of Necessity," *Journal of the Abraham Lincoln Association*, Vol. 18, No. 1, 57-81.

85 "Meditation on the Divine Will," Basler, *Collected Works*, Volume 5, 403-404.

86 Ibid.

87 Second Inaugural Address, Basler, *Collected Works*, Volume 8, 332-333.

88 Quoted by Lloyd Lewis, *Myths After Lincoln*, (NY: 1929), 344.

89 Mary B. Clay Botkin, in the *Lexington Herald*, via Katherine Helm, 241-243.

90 Herndon, *Herndon's Lincoln*, (Cleveland, 1949), 454; also see Noah Brooks, "Personal Recollections of Abraham Lincoln," *Harper's Monthly*, July, 1865, 224.

91 Julia Taft Bayne, ibid, 77-78.

Chapter 13

92 Larry Dossey, MD, *The Power of Premonition*, New York: Dutton, 2009; 27.

93 Julia Taft Bayne, *Tad Lincoln's Father*, 179.

94 Ward Hill Lamon, *Recollections*, 115.

95 Fehrenbach and Fehrenbach, 78; Le Grand B. Cannon, *Reminiscences*, 174; Wilson and Davis, *HI*, 679.

96 Mary Ben Harden Helm, *The True Story of Mary, Wife of Lincoln*, (NY, 1928), 227.

97 Ibid.

98 Julia Taft Bayne, ibid, 131-132.

99 "Note of June 9, 1863," Basler, *Collected Works*, Volume 6.

100 Wilson and Davis, (Herndon's Interview with Mary Todd Lincoln), September 1866, *HI*, No. 254, 359.

101 Ron Musa, PhD., "President Abraham Lincoln's Prophetic Dreams," http://Psychology.artcileberry.com.

102 Webb Garrison, *The Lincoln No One Knows*, 251.

Chapter 14

103 Jay Monaghan, "Was Abraham Lincoln Really a Spiritualist?" *Journal of the Illinois State Historical Society*, Vol. 34, No. 2 (June 1941), 209.

104 Book of Samuel I, Chapter 28, 3-25; St. Augustine, De Cura pro Mortuis.

105 "Spiritualism," Paul S. Boyer, *Oxford Companion to United States History*, (NY: Oxford University Press, 2001). (After Howell's book *Undiscovered Country*)

106 Princess Salm-Salm, *Ten Years of My Life*, (Detroit: Belford Brothers, 1877), 45.

107 *The Herald of Progress*, January 11, 1862.

108 *Freeborn County Standard*, (Albert Lea, Minnesota), September 30, 1893.

109 *Daily Republican*, October 24, 1891.

110 Colonel Bundy, in *Idaho Daily Statesman*, (Boise City, Idaho), October 24, 1891, (after a report in a Chicago paper); Colonel Bundy was Editor of the *Religio-Philosophical Journal*, a Chicago Spiritualist periodical.

111 Colonel Kase, "How Lincoln Came to Issue his Emancipation Proclamation," in Mrs. W. E. Williams, *Abraham Lincoln, A Spiritualist*. (pamphlet) (NY, n.d.)

112 For Kase's narratives see: Williams, *Abraham Lincoln*, ibid; "Was Mr. Lincoln a Spiritualist?" *New York Evening Sun*, November 23, 1894; Emma Hardinge Britten, *Nineteenth Century Miracles*, (NY: Lovell & Co., 1884), 484-87.

113 "I. B. Conklin [sic] to Abraham Lincoln," Saturday, December 28, 1861. Library of Congress, Abraham Lincoln Papers, Series I. General Correspondence, 1833-1916.

114 *Waukesha Freeman*, (Waukesha, Wisconsin), March 12, 1861 (after an article in the *Cleveland Plaindealer*).

115 Lecture by Emma Hardinge Britten before the London Dialectic Society, delivered February 2, 1869. *Report on Spiritualism*, (London, 1873), 111-112.

116 "G.A.A Wide Awake to Abraham Lincoln," Tuesday, December 11, 1860, Library of Congress, Abraham Lincoln Papers, Series I, General Correspondence, 1833-1916.

117 Wayne C. Temple, "Herndon on Lincoln: An Unknown Interview with a List of Books in the Lincoln and Herndon Law Office." *Journal of the Illinois State Historical Society*, Volume 98, 1-2 (Spring, 2005), 38-39; Robert Bray, "What Abraham Lincoln Read—an Evaluation and Annotated list." *Journal of the Abraham Lincoln Association*, Vol. 28, No. 2 (Summer, 2007), Table 3.

118 "J. B. Hastings to Abraham Lincoln," August 9, 1861, Library of Congress, Abraham Lincoln Papers, Series 1. General Correspondence. 1833-1916.

119 For more details on the Reverend Laurie and the New York Avenue Presbyterian Church, see "New York Avenue Presbyterian Church" at www.mrlincolnswhitehouse.org.

120 Information on the Laurie family is via Ancestry. com; Geneology.com/GenForum; and "Interments in the Historic Congressional Cemetery" at bytesofhistory.com.

121 Notarized Statement of Jack Laurie, dated November 1, 1885, in Cyrus Oliver Poole, "The Religious Convictions of Abraham Lincoln, A Study," *Religio-Philosophical Journal*, November 28, 1885; accessed online at www.seekeronline.org.

122 Ervin Chapman, *Latest Light on Abraham Lincoln and Wartime Memories, II*, (NY: F. H. Revell, 1917), 505.

123 Dr. Fayette Hall, *Copperhead*, (New Haven: self-published, 1902), 37.

124 Warren Chase, "Defense of Spiritualism," *The Liberator*, January 8, 1858, 7; also see *The Liberator*, January 1, 1858, 4, and July 23, 1858, 119. Chase, a relative of Lincoln's Secretary of Treasury, was a noted Wisconsin reformer, advocating women's rights, temperance, Socialism, and racial equality as well as Spiritualism.

Chapter 15

125 Irving Stone, "Mary Todd Lincoln, a Final Judgment," *Abraham Lincoln Monograph* (Springfield, IL: Abraham Lincoln Association, 1973).

126 David Herbert Donald, *Lincoln*, (NY, 1996).

127 See www.mrlincolnswhitehouse.org; the site is maintained by the Lincoln Institute.

128 Margaret Leech, *Reveille in Washington, 1860-1865*, (NY and London, 1941), 305.

129 See the article "Mary's Charlatans" at www. mrlincolnswhitehouse.org.

130 "Roster of the 16th Connecticut Regiment, Volunteer Infantry," compiled by Scott W. Holmes, Civil War Plymouth Pilgrims Descendants Society, Feb. 12, 1997; accessed via US Gen Web (http: //files. usgwarchives.org/ct/statewide/military/ civilwar/rost001atxt) on 7/17/11; also

cf. Janet B. Hewett (Ed.), *The Roster of Union Soldiers*.

131 Colburn, ibid, 27.

132 Colburn, ibid, 29.

133 Ibid.

134 On resistance to the Emancipation Declaration, see James M. McPherson, *Battle Cry of Freedom* (NY: Oxford U. Press, 1988), 360, 594-95, and Allen C. Guelzo, "Defending Emancipation: Abraham Lincoln and the Conkling Letter, 1863," *Civil War History*, Volume 48 (December 2002), 313.

135 Cf. Gary E. Wait, "Gideon Welles—Glastonbury's Native Son," Historical Society of Glastonbury, via Welles Family Association (www.wellesfamily.com, accessed July 8, 2011).

136 See "Introduction" by Frances Smith Foster, Editor, in *Elizabeth Keckley, Behind the Scenes* or *Thirty Years a Slave and Four Years in the White House*, Lakeside Classics Series, Volume 96; Chicago: RR Donnelly, 1998.

137 Colburn, ibid, 26.

138 "A Citizen of Ohio" (David Quinn), *Interior Causes of the War: The Nation Demonized and the President a Spirit Rapper* (NY, 1863), 6.

139 David Quinn, ibid; also "Envisioning the Civil War" (http://www.spirithistory. com/war.html).

140 "The President Declared a Convert to Spiritualism," *Daily Evening Bulletin*, (San Francisco, CA) April 1, 1863 (issue 148).

141 Theodore Calvin Pease (Ed.), *The Diary of Orville Hickman Browning*, (Chicago: 1927), Volume II, 608-09.

142 Colburn, ibid, 30-34; Colonel Simon P. Kase, "How Lincoln Came to Issue His Emancipation Proclamation," in Mrs. M. E. Williams, *Abraham Lincoln a Spiritualist*; "Was Mr. Lincoln a Spiritualist?" *New York Evening Sun*, November 23, 1894; *The Galveston Daily News* (Houston, TX) August 3, 1891 (issue 132), 5. As noted before, Colonel Kase's chronology is off, but the incidents he witnessed correlate with Nettie's more accurate narrative and several secondary accounts. On the discrepancies in Colonel Kase's narratives, see Dr. Walter Franklin Prince, "The Aetiology of a Psychical Legend," *Psypioneer Journal*, 30-36, and Paul Gaunt's rejoinder in the same issue.

143 Colburn, ibid, 50.

144 "Joshua F. Speed to Abraham Lincoln, Monday, October 26, 1863," Abraham Lincoln Papers at the Library of Congress, Series I. General Correspondence. 1833-1916.

145 Colburn, ibid, 41-42.

146 See "A Chat with a Spiritualist," *New York Times*, July 28, 1872; Naumkeag Notations, "Salem's Psychic Past Lives," *Salem Gazette*, Oct. 19, 2006.

147 Thomas Coulson, *Joseph Henry, His life and Works*, 308-309.

148 Noah Brooks, (Herbert Mitgang, Ed.), *Washington in Lincoln's Time*, 66-68.

149 Nettie Colburn Maynard, *Was Lincoln a Spiritualist?*, First Edition, 263-64.

150 "The Colchester Case: Why the Spiritualist is Not a Juggler," *New York Times*, September 3, 1865.

151 (Prior Melton), "Spiritualism in the White House," *Boston Gazette*, April 23, 1863; reprinted in *The New York Herald*, May 30, 1863, 4, and *The Herald of Progress* (New York), May 1863, with by-line and the headline "A Readable Sketch." A selectively edited version is reprinted in *Ferhrenbach & Fehrenbach*, 10-11. *The New York Herald* also had an editorial on page 6 of the same issue commenting on the Shockle séance, subtitled, "The New Religious Philosophy."

152 See introductory comments, "Spiritualism at the White House," http://www.spirithistory.com/whthouse.html

153 See Mitch Horowitz, *Occult America*, (NY, 2009), 60.

154 Gary Pendle, "Einstein's Close Encounter," *The Manchester Guardian* (UK), July 14, 2005 (accessed online at http://www.guardian.co.uk/science/2005/jul/14/3/print)

155 "Lincoln and Mediums," *Rocky Mountain News*, October 20, 1891; variants of the same article were published in the *Atchison Champion*, October 20, 1891, and the *Milwaukee Sentinel*.

156 Colburn, ibid, 6.

157 "John W. Edmonds to Abraham Lincoln," Monday, June 1, 1863. Library of Congress, Abraham Lincoln Papers, Series I. General Correspondence. 1833-1916. In the same archive is Senator Edwin D. Morgan's cover letter to Lincoln that accompanied Edmonds' package. For Lincoln's acknowledgement of receipt of the books, see Basler, *Collected Works of Abraham Lincoln*, Volume 7, 133.

Chapter 16

158 Ward Hill Lamon, *Recollections*, 114-117, 120.

Chapter 17

159 Gideon Welles, *Diary of Gideon Welles*, (Boston & NY: Houghton Mifflin, 1911), Volume II, 282-83; Frederick W. Seward, *Reminiscences of a Wartime Statesman and Diplomat, 1830-1915*

(NY: G. P. Putnam, 1916), 255.

160 Lamon, *Recollections*, 120.

161 Lamon, *Recollections*, 118.

162 Welles, *Diary*, footnote, 283; Grant, *Personal Memoirs*, 750; his own presentiment, Grant, 33; For Julia Grant's presentiments on April 14, Julia Dent Grant, *The Personal Memoirs of Julia Dent Grant*, 154-156; also see 76, 78, 93, 157-158 for Mrs. Grant's other presentiments. On the Grants' publicly known faith in the paranormal, see General Adam Bodeau, "The Last Days of General Grant," *Century Magazine*, Vol. 30, No. 6 (October 1885), 935.

Chapter 18

163 "Mrs. Lincoln's Presentiment," *New York Times*, May 1, 1865, 5.

164 Marquis de Chambron, ibid, 35; Lloyd Lewis, 42.

165 Marquis de Chambron, ibid, 32.

166 Julia Dent Grant, *The Personal Memoirs of Julia Dent Grant* (NY: Putnams, 1975), 155-56.

167 William H. Crook, *Through Five Administrations, Reminiscences of Colonel William H. Crook* (NY, Harper, 1910), 66-67.

168 Benjamin Quarles, *The Negro in the Civil War*, (Boston, 1953), 340.

169 Major George Putnam was the affluent scion of the founder of G. P. Putnam and Sons, the famed New York publishing house. George was one of the "sons" in the corporate title.

170 George Haven Putnam, *Abraham Lincoln the Great Captain: Personal Reminisces of a Veteran of the Civil War.* (Lecture delivered at Oxford University, May 3, 1928), (Oxford, 1928), 28-30.

Chapter 19

171 Emanuel Hertz, *The Hidden Lincoln*, (NY, Blur Ribbon Books, 1940): 17-18.

172 For a general biography of Robert Todd Lincoln, see John S. Goff, *Robert Todd Lincoln: A Man in his Own Right* (Norman, OK: University of Oklahoma Press, 1968); U.S. Army Center for Military History, *Secretaries of War and Secretaries of the Army.* A recent survey of the post assassination misfortunes of the Lincoln clan are now chronicled in Charles Lachman's *The Last Lincolns, The Rise and Fall of a Great American Family* (NY: Union Square Press, 2010).

Chapter 20

173 "The Spirits at the White House," *Atlanta Constitution*, September 13, 1868.

174 "White House Servants," *Arkansas Democrat*

(Little Rock, Arkanasas), March 21, 1899, 3, Column B.

175 Gary Walter (White House Usher), "Ask the White House," October 31, 2007 (http://georgewbush-whitehouse.archives.gov/ask/print/20031031-2.html)

176 Sara Nelson, "Fright House," *London Daily Mail Online*, November 5, 2009

177 Joan P. Gage, "President Reagan's White House Ghost Story," Open Salon.com, October 20, 2009; also see "A Ghost in the White House? The Lincoln Bedroom," Abraham Lincoln's Research Site, (file://A:Hauntings of Lincoln Bedroom_files\Lincoln54.htm) accessed 4/6/2001.

178 Yvette La Pierre, "Favorite Haunts," National Parks, November-December, 1994, 44-46.

179 Cf. "The Westbound Train Going Home," Christopher Kiernan Coleman, *Ghosts and Haunts of the Civil War*, (Nashville, TN: Rutledge Hill Press, 1999), 151-155.

180 Breanne Parcels, "UU Mythbusters Investigate Lincoln Train," *The Urbana Daily Citizen*, June 5, 2001; Anon., "Ghostly Lincoln Funeral Train," Paranormal Studies forum on Above Top Secret website (www.abovetopsecret.com/forum/thread107433/pg1) December 27-30, 2004.

181 Cf. Merlin Jones, *Haunted Places* (Boca Raton, 1999), 35-36.

182 "The Equinox, Manchester, Vt." The Shadowlands: Famous Hauntings website (http://famousplaces.ghosthunting101.com/equinox.htm) accessed 11/1/2001.

183 Troy Taylor, "The Lincoln Home: Is it Really Haunted?" (www.illinoishauntings.com/president.html), Prairie Ghosts website, 1997.

184 Anon. "The Ghost of Abraham Lincoln." Legends of America website (www.legendsofamerica.com/il-hauntedspringield.html).

Chapter 21

185 Ward Hill Lamon, *Recollections*, 121.

186 Ibid.

187 John T. Stuart in Herndon, *Life*, 473.

188 Charles Dickens, in a letter dated February 4, 1868, to John Forster, his biographer, cited by James Coates, *Seeing the Invisible* (NY: Fowler & Wells, 1906), 225; Dickens also told the story to Queen Victoria: Arthur Henry Beaven, *Popular Royalty* (London: Sampson Low Marston, 1904), 225.

189 Wilson and Davis, *HI*, 458.

190 Iris Owen and Margaret Sparrow, *Conjuring up Philip: An Adventure in Psycho-Kinesis* (NY: Pocket Books, 1977).

191 Coast to Coast Radio Interview with Mitch Horowitz, April 7, 2005. (transcript at http://www.mitchhorowitz.com/understanding-the-occult.html)

Archives and Libraries Consulted

Family Search.org
Gutenburg Project
Internet Archive (www.archive.org)
Library of Congress (LC)
Nashville Public Library, Main Branch (NPL)
National Archives (NARAS)
Tennessee State Library and Archives
(TSLA)

Newspapers Consulted

Arkansas Democrat
Atlanta Constitution
Biloxi Sun Herald
Chicago Tribune
Galveston daily News
Milwaukee Sentinel
New Orleans Daily Picayune
New York Evening Sun
New York Mercury
New York Times
Rocky Mountain News, Denver
Wisconsin State Register

Articles

Alter, Emily. "The Spiritualist Movement and its Advancement of the Nineteenth Century Women's Movement." *The Concord Review* 11, No. 3 (Spring, 2001): 167-192.

Anon. "The Statue of Freedom," Wikipedia entry.

Bodeau, General Adam. "The Last Days of General Grant." *Century Magazine* 30, No. 6 (October, 1885): 935.

Boritt, Gabor S. and Adam Boritt. "Lincoln and Marfan Syndorme, the Medical Diagnosis of a Historical Figure." *Civil War History*, Vol. 29, No. 3 (September 1983), 213-229.

Bray, Robert. "What Abraham Lincoln Read—An Evaluation and Annotated List." *Journal of the Abraham Lincoln Association*, Vol. 28, No. 2 (Summer 2007).

Brooks, Noah. "Personal Recollections of Abraham Lincoln." *Harper's New Monthly Magazine*, July 1865, 222-230.

Buckley, J.M. "Presentiments, Visions, and Apparitions." *Century Magazine*, Vol. 38, No. 3 (July, 1889), 453-467.

Bulkeley, Keith, PhD. "Abraham Lincoln's Dreams." Dream Research and Education blog (http://kellybulkeley.co/abraham-lincoln), posted December 5, 2009.

Crotty, Rob. "The Curious Case of Robert Lincoln."

Prologue: Pieces of History, (E-zine of the National Archives) (http://blogs.archive.gove/prologue/?p=2239)

de Chambron, Marquis (Charles A. Pineton). "Personal Recollections of Mr. Lincoln." *Scribner's Magazine*, Vol. 43, No. 1 (January 1893), 26-38.

Fair, Susan. "Spiritualism and the Civil War." *The Gettysburg Experience* (online edition: www.thegettysburgexperience.com/pas_issue_headlines/2010/October/spiritualism.html

Finacom, Steven. "Lincoln, a Comet and the Politics of a Nation Divided." *The Berkeley Daily Planet*, October 2, 2009.

Gage, Joan P. "President Reagan's White House Ghost Story." Open Salon.com, October 30, 2009 (online archive).

Gamut, Paul J. "Dr. Walter Franklin Prince vs. Simon P. Kase." *Psypioneer*, Vol. 6, No. 2, February 2010).

Grimsley, Elizabeth Todd. "Six Months in the White House." *Journal of the Illinois State Historical Society*, Vol. 15, No. 3/4 : 42-73.

Guelzo, Allen C. "Abraham Lincoln and the Doctrine of Necessity." *Journal of the Abraham Lincoln Association*, Vol. 18, No. 1: 57-81.

"Defending Emancipation: Abraham Lincoln and the Conkling Letter, 1863." *Civil War History*, Vol. 48, No. 4 (December 2002): 313-337.

Horowitz, Mitch. Interview, Coast to Coast radio show, April 7, 2005. (Transcript accessed via www.mitchhorowitz.com)

Isbell, Tim. "Capitol Dome Serves as Symbol of Unity." *Biloxi Sun-Herald*, (online edition). June 13, 2011.

"J.C.H.: Predestined Presidents." *New York Times*, December 29, 1912.

Jordan, Philip D. "Skulls, Rappers, Ghosts and Doctors." *Ohio Archaeological and Historical Quarterly* 53, No. 4 (October-December, 1994), 339-354.

Kempf, Edward J. MD. "Abraham Lincoln's Organic and Emotional Neurosis." *AMA Archives of Neurology and Psychiatry*, Vol. 67, No. 4 (April 1952), 419-433.

Lamon, Ward Hill. "Abraham Lincoln's Strange Dream: His Singular Philosophy in Regard to Dreams and Presentiments." *Chicago Daily News*, August 27, 1887.

Lang, Andrew. "Second Sight." *Enccyclopaedia*

Britannica, 11th Edition. Cambridge, England: Cambridge University, 1910-1911.

Martinez, Susan, PhD. "Lincoln and the Afterlife." *Atlantis Rising*, 69 (May-June, 2008).

Masa, Ron PhD. "President Abraham Lincoln's Prophetic Dream that Foretold his Own Death in the White House." February 12, 2010, accessed at http://psychology.articleberry.com website.

Melton, Prior. "A Readable Sketch: Spiritualism at the White House." *Herald of Progress* (NY, May 1863), 8. (Reprint of *Boston Gazette* article about Shockle séance with by-line.)

Monaghan, Jay. "Was Lincoln Really a Spiritualist?" *Journal of the Illinois State Historical Society*, Vol. 34, No. 2 (June 1941), 209-232.

Nickell, Joe. "Paranormal Lincoln." *Skeptical Inquirer*, May 1999 (accessed online 3/29/2001 via CISCOP online archive).

Olson, Donald W. and Laurie E. Jasinski. "Abraham Lincoln's Celestial Connections." *Sky and Telescope*, Vol. 117, No. 3 (March 2009), 66.

Pendle, George. "Einstein's Close Encounter." *The Manchester Guardian*, July 14, 2005 (www.guardian.co.uk/science).

Price, Leslie. "Abraham Lincoln, Spiritualism and Emancipation." *Psyppioneer* 1, No. 4 (August 2004): 25-27.

Prince, Dr. Walter Franklin. "The Aetiology of a 'Psychical' Legend." *Psypioneer Journal*, Vol. 6, No. 2 (February 2010), 30-36.

Putnam, Major George Haven. "Abraham Lincoln the Great Captain: Personal Reminiscences of a Veteran of the Civil War." Lecture delivered at Oxford, May 3, 1928; 32-page pamphlet.

Robbins, Peggy. "The Lincolns and Spiritualism," *Civil War Times Illustrated*, Vol. 15, No. 5 (August,1976), 5, 6, 8-10, 46, 47.

Spangler, Michael. "Benjamin Brown French in the Lincoln Period." *White House History*, No. 8 (Journal of the White House Historical Association).

Stone, Irving. "Mary Todd Lincoln: A Final Judgment?" *Lincoln Monographs* (address given before annual banquet of Abraham Lincoln Association). Springfield, Illinois: Abraham Lincoln Association, 1973.

Stuart, Nancy Rubin. "The Raps Heard Around the World." *American History*, August, 2005, 42-48, 78, 80.

Sunfellow, David. "Parting Visions." New Heaven New Earth website (http://www.nhne.com/articles/sapartingvisions.html), January 6, 1995. (Article is based on the research of Dr. Melvin Morse, MD.)

Temple, Wayne C. "Herndon on Lincoln: An Unknown Interview, with a List of Books in the Lincoln and Herndon Law Office." *Journal of the Illinois State Historical Society*, Vol. 48, No. 1/2 (Spring 2005), 34-50.

Trainor, Joseph. "1863: The President's Psychic." *UFO Roundup*, Vol. 7, No. 8 (February 19, 2002).

Wait, Gary E. "Gideon Welles—Glastonbury's Native Son" (monograph). Glastonbury, CT: Historical Society of Glastonbury, n.d.

Walter, Gary. Interview, October 31, 2003, White House online forum (accessed via georgebush-whitehouse Archives).

Ward, Paul et al. "The Morbid Curse of Robert Todd Lincoln." Snopes forums, History Archive (msgboard.snopes.com), November 2-4, 2001.

Widmer, Ted. "Land Pirate." "Disunion" blog, Opinionator, NY Times.com, April 26, 2011. (http://opionator.blogs.nytimes.com/category/disunion/)

Williams, Mrs. M. E. (Ed.), (Col. Kase). "How Lincoln Came to Issue his Emancipation Proclamation." *Abraham Lincoln a Spiritualist* (Pamphlet). (New York, n.d.)

Wilson, Douglas L. "Keeping Lincoln's Secrets." *Atlantic Monthly*, Vol. 285, No. 5, May 2000, 78-88.

Books

Arnold, Isaac N. *The Life of Lincoln*. Chicago, Illinois: Jansen McClung, 1885.

Aswell, James R. (Ed.). *God Bless the Devil: Liars' Bench Tales*. Knoxville, Tennessee: UT Press, 1985 (1940 orig. edtion).

Basler, Roy P. (Ed.) *Collected Works of Abraham Lincoln, 1809-1865*. 8 Vols. New Brunswick, New Jersey: Rutgers U. Press, 1953.

Bayne, Julia Taft. *Tad Lincoln's Father*. Boston, Massachusetts: Little, Brown, 1931.

Blakeslee, B. F. *History of the 16th Regiment Connecticut Volunteer Infantry*. Hartford, Connecticut: Case, Lockwood, and Brainard, Co., 1875.

Boyer, Paul S. *Oxford Companion to United States History*. New York, New York: Oxford University Press, 2001.

Bronte, Charlotte. *Jane Eyre*. New York, New York: Penguin, 1966 (orig. pub. 1847).

Brooks, Noah. *Washington in Lincoln's Time*. New York, New York: Century, 1895.

Campanella, Richard. *Lincoln in New Orleans: The*

1828-1831 Flatboat Voyages and their place in History. Lafayette, Louisiana: University of Louisiana at Lafayette, 2010.

Carpenter, Frank. *Six Months at the White House with Abraham Lincoln*. New York, New York: Hurd & Houghton, 1866.

Chapman, Ervin S. *Latest Light on Abraham Lincoln and War-Time Memories*, 2 Vols. New York, New York: F. H. Revell, 1917.

Chase, Salmon P. (Samuel H. Dobson, Comp). *Diary and Correspondence*, 2 Vols. Annual Report, American Historical Assoc., 1902. Washington, D.C.: American History Association, 1903.

Coulson, Thomas. *Joseph Henry, His Life and Works*. Princeton, New Jersey: Princeton University Press, 1950.

Cox, Robert S. *Body and Soul*. Charlottesville, Virginia: University of Virginia Press, 2003.

Crook, Colonel William H. *Through Five Administrations, Reminiscences of Colonel William H. Crook*. New York & London: Harper Brothers, 1910.

Current, Richard N. *The Lincoln Nobody Knows*. New York, New York: Hill and Wang, 1958.

Donald, David H. *Lincoln's Herndon*. New York, New York: DaCapo, 1989 (orig. pub. 1948).

Dossey, Larry M.D. *The Power of Premonitions*. New York, New York: Dutton, 2009.

Eaton, John and Ethel Osgood Mason. *Grant, Lincoln and the Freedmen: Reminiscences of the Civil War*. New York, New York: Longmans, 1907.

Eliade, Mircea. *Shamanism: Archaic Techniques of Ecstasy*. Princeton, New Jersey: Princeton University Press, 1972.

Fehrenbacher, Don E. and Virginia Fehrenbacher (Compilers). *Recollected Words of Abraham Lincoln*. Stanford, Connecticut: Stanford University Press, 1996.

Garrison, Webb. *The Lincoln No One Knows*. Nashville, Tennessee: Rutledge Hill Press, 1993.

Goodwin, Doris Kearns. *A Team of Rivals: the Political Genius of Abraham Lincoln*. New York, New York: Simon & Schuster, 2005.

Gordon, General John, CSA. *Reminiscences of the Civil War*. New York, New York: Scribners,1903.

Grant, Julia Dent. *The Personal Memoirs of Julia Dent Grant*. New York, New York: Putnam,1975.

Grant, Ulysses S. *Personal Memoirs*, 2 Vols. New York, New York: Putnam, 1990 (originally publ. 1885).

Hall, Dr. Fayette. *The Copperhead: or, the Secret Political History of our Civil War Unveiled*. New Haven, Connecticut: self published, 1902.
Secret Political History of the War of the Rebellion. New Haven, Connecticut: self published, 1890.

Haskins, Jim. *Voodoo and Hoodoo*. New York, New York: Stein & Day, 1981.

Helm, Katherine (Comp.). *The True Story of Mary, Wife of Lincoln*. New York, New York: Harper & Bro., 1928.

Herndon, William Henry and Jesse Weik. *Herndon's Lincoln: The True Story of a Great Life*, 3 Vols. Springfield, Illinois: Herndon's Lincoln Publishing Co., 1921.
Life of Lincoln. Cleveland, Ohio: World Publishing Co., 1949.

Hertz, Emanuel. *The Hidden Lincoln: From the Letters and Papers of W. H. Herndon*. New York, New York: Blue Ribbon Books, 1940.

Hewitt, Janet B., Editor. *The Roster of Union Soldiers, 1861-1865*. Wilmington, North Carolina: Broadfoot, 1977.

Horowitz, Mitch. *Occult America*. New York, New York: Bantam, 2009.

Lamon, Ward Hill. *Recollections of Abraham Lincoln, 1847-1865*. Washington, D.C.: pub. by the editor, 1911.

Lee, Richard M. *Mr. Lincoln's City: An Illustrated Guide to the Civil War Sites of Washington*. McLean, Virginia: EPM Publishing, 1981.

Leech, Margaret. *Reveille in Washington, 1860-1865*. New York, New York: Harper & Bro., 1941; Garden City, Doubleday: 1945.

Lewis, Lloyd. *Myths After Lincoln*. Gloucester, Massachusetts: P. Smith, 1973 (first edition, published in 1929).

Maynard, Nettie Colburn. *Was Abraham Lincoln a Spiritualist?* Philadelphià, Pennsylvania: H. C. Hartranft, 1891 (first edition).
Was Abraham Lincoln a Spiritualist? Chicago, Illinois: Progressive Thinker, 1917 (second, abridged edition).

McClure, Colonel Alexander K. *"Abe" Lincoln's Yarns and Stories*. Chicago & Philadelphia: John C. Winston, 1904.

McPherson, James M. *Battle Cry of Freedom*. New York, New York: Oxford, 1988.

Moody, Dr. Raymond A. Jr. M.D. *Life After Life*. St. Simons Island, South Carolina: Mockingbird Books, 1975.

Owen, Iris and Margaret Sparrow. *Conjuring Up Philip: an Adventure in Psycho-kinesis*. New York, New York: Pocket Books, 1977.

Pease, Thomas, Editor. *Diary of Orville H. Browning*. Chicago, Illinois: Illinois State

Historical Library, 1927. (Collections of the Illinois State Historical Library, Vol. XX; Lincoln Series, Vol. II).

Pillsbury, Albert E. *Lincoln and Slavery*. Boston & New York: Houghton Mifflin, 1903.

Quarles, Benjamin. *The Negro in the Civil War*. Boston, Massachusetts: Little Brown, 1953.

Quinn, David. "A Citizen of Ohio." *Interior Causes of the War: The Nation Divided and its President a Spirit Rapper*. New York, New York: M. Doolady, 1863.

Randall, Ruth Painter. *Mary Lincoln: Biography of a Marriage*. Boston, Massachusetts: Little Brown, 1953.

Rawick, George P., Editor. *The American Slave, a Composite Autobiography*. Westport, Connecticut: Greenwood Press, 2000.

Salm-Salm, Princess. *Ten Years of My Life*. Detroit, Michigan: Belford Brothers, 1877.

Sandburg, Carl. *Abraham Lincoln the Prairie Years and the War Years*. New York, New York: Houghton Mifflin Harcourt, 2002.

Schurz, Carl. *Reminiscences of Carl Schurz*, 3 Vols. New York, New York: Methuen, 1907-1908.

Sarcher, Victor. *The Farewell to Lincoln*. Nashville, Tennessee: Abingdon Press, 1965.

Seward, Frederick W. *Reminiscences of a War-Time Statesman and Diplomat, 1830-1915*. New York, New York: G. P. Putnam, 1916.

Steiger, Brad E. *Gale Encyclopedia of the Unusual and Unexplained*. Farmington Heights, Michigan: Gale, 2003.

Taft, Horatio Nelson (1806-88). *Diary, 1861-65*, 3 Vols. Library of Congress, Wash. D.C. (online at American Memory).

Welles, Gideon. *Diary of Gideon Welles*, 3 Vols. Boston & New York: Houghton Mifflin, 1911 (reprinted 1966).

Wilson, Douglas L. and Rodney Davis. *Herndon's Informants*. Champaign, Illinois: University of Illinois Press, 1997.